AiR iS ALL OXYGEN

Essential Science
You Should Have Learned ...
But Probably Didn't!

Bill Morelan, Ph.D.

Printed in the United States
ISBN: 978-1-500389-01-7

- - -

Cover Photo: Marena Holloway Photography
Photo Editing: Joshua Ray
Model: Michael Bascue

Editors: Talena Keeler, Jamie Massey
Science Consultant: Tina South

Table of Contents

**To my daughter Jamie,
who thought plasma TVs required
human blood.**

National Standards

Fundamental concepts in this book are based on
the National Science Education Standards (1996) and
the Next Generation Science Standards (2013).
These foundational references outline essential science content,
and almost every state uses either one or the other.

More information can be found at:
http://www.nap.edu/openbook.php?record_id=4962
http://www.nextgenscience.org/

Introduction

In June of 1190, Holy Roman Emperor Frederick I was on his 3rd Crusade to recapture the Holy Land. After days of marching through the parched desert, his army arrived at the Saleph river. Soaked with sweat and too impatient to cross the crowded bridge, he decided to swim his horse across the river. Unfortunately, Frederick was wearing a full suit of armor at the time. You can guess the rest.*

Scientific Literacy

While we shake our heads at Frederick's inability to understand basic science, somehow our own education (or lack of it)** has left many of us scientifically illiterate.

Scientific literacy, the ability to think and speak intelligently about scientific topics, is more than just a way to amaze and amuse our friends. It cuts to the core of our ability to make intelligent decisions. In many ways, the inability to understand basic science can be as much a handicap as an inability to read and write. Here are some examples ...

In 1992, the book *Sharks Don't Get Cancer* was hailed as a breakthrough in the prevention and treatment of cancer. Sales of shark cartilage extract skyrocketed. Millions of dollars were spent. But according to David Shiffman, a shark researcher at the University of Miami, "Sharks *do* get cancer ... Even if they didn't, eating shark products won't cure cancer any more than me eating Michael Jordan would make me better at basketball."[1]

Busts of Frederick often have a rather surprised expression.
**You may have thought you had better things to do in school than study.*

In 2012, headlines proclaimed, "Coffee Makes You Live Longer!" Since most of us want to believe our habits are healthy,* the urge to believe the reports quickly outran the facts. The "proof" came from a single study reported in the *New England Journal of Medicine* [2] where researchers found a correlation between longevity and coffee drinking. But the population studied was very specific — people who were at least 50, had no history of cancer, heart disease, or stroke, and didn't smoke. And several important risk factors such as participants' socio-economic status, access to health care, cholesterol levels, or family medical history, were not part of the study. To be fair, both the researchers and the journal's editor pointed out these limitations and advised caution. But that didn't prevent the idea that "they've proven drinking coffee is good for you" from permeating society.

More recently, you've probably noticed that many discussions on global warming seem to have more to do with politics than with science. You can often predict a person's views on this topic based on their political leanings. While this may or may not have serious consequences for your future**, few would argue with the fact that discussions based on scientific evidence usually result in better solutions than discussions based solely on opinions.

In short, a solid grounding in science helps us avoid what Issac Asimov called "the false notion that democracy means my ignorance is just as good as your knowledge."

Common Misconceptions

Scientific misconceptions are everywhere! Some seem logical, some are funny, others are downright dangerous. In a few cases, what you don't know can kill you! (See the first example on the next page.) Here are some common misconceptions:

Personally, I'm looking for a metastudy that says chocolate is a great diet food.
**unless you live in Florida*

- *Lightning never strikes twice in the same place.*

  Lightning often strikes twice in the same place! For example, the **Empire State Building** gets struck over 100 times a year.

- *Seasons are caused by the Earth being closer to the Sun in the summer than in the winter.*

  Seasons are not caused by the Earth's distance from the Sun. In fact, the Earth is the *farthest* from the Sun when it's summer in the Northern Hemisphere. Seasons are caused by Earth's tilted axis, which affects the amount of direct sunlight a given area receives. More direct sunlight equals more heat.

- *Objects float because they are lighter than water.*

  Not exactly. Ships can weigh thousands of tons. Floating is actually related to displacement (the weight of both the object and the weight of the water it displaces). In general, an object must weigh less than the water it displaces in order to float.

- *Magnets are strongly attracted to all metals.*

  Oops! What about aluminum, copper, tin, and lead?   On the other hand, there are some non-metallic substances (like super cold liquid oxygen) that attract magnets, too.

- *Air and oxygen are the same thing.*

  Many people believe that humans breathe in oxygen and exhale carbon dioxide. But what we're actually breathing in are Earth's atmospheric gases ... commonly referred to as "air." And air is only about 21% oxygen. The rest of air is mostly inert nitrogen.* Thus, ***Air Is Not Oxygen***.

*which only aliens in B-rated movies breathe

Disclaimer

Many of the concepts in this book have been simplified for clarity. You'll require a much more complex understanding if you plan to win a Nobel prize!* But **Air Is Not Oxygen** *can* help you gain a clearer understanding of basic science concepts. And once you have the basics, everything else begins to fall into place.

You'll have a lot more "ah ha!" moments. You'll begin to see connections to other disciplines. You'll have the foundation to dig deeper into those things that interest you most. (Whole careers have been built on that!)

So, enjoy the journey. Read a chapter or two and ponder what you've discovered. Underline, highlight, and make little stars. Have fun with the hands-on activities and learn by doing.

Who knows where your journey will end?

Bill Morelan
Byrd's on Mulberry

*unless you develop "cold fusion" in your garage ...
and I' don't mean freezing a Ford!*

- - -

REFERENCES

[1] "Forget the Myth: Sharks do get Cancer!" Retrieved July 3, 2014 from: http://www.nbcnews.com/science/science-news/forget-myth-sharks-do-get-cancer-even-great-whites-f2D11703500

[2] "Association of Coffee Drinking with Total and Cause-Specific Mortality" Neal D. Freedman, Ph.D., Yikyung Park, Sc.D., Christian C. Abnet, Ph.D., Albert R. Hollenbeck, Ph.D., and Rashmi Sinha, Ph.D. N Engl J Med 2012; 366:1891-1904 May 17, 2012DOI: 10.1056/NEJMoa1112010. Retrieved July 18, 2014 from: http://well.blogs.nytimes.com/2012/05/16/coffee-drinkers-may-live-longer/?_php=true&_type=blogs&_r=0

Physical Science

"We can lick gravity ... but sometimes the paperwork is overwhelming!"

– Wernher von Braun

Preview

Set an ice cube in a small dish beside you as you work. Glance over at it occasionally as it melts. Eventually, it will become a pool of water. Wait long enough, and the water will disappear.

This simple exercise demonstrates the three most fundamental forms (or "states") of matter on Earth.

Essential Concepts

You probably learned about these "three states of matter" when you were in school. Remember — solid, liquid, gas?

Actually, there's a fourth fundamental state of matter called plasma.* But even though it was first discovered in 1879, it didn't start appearing in most textbooks until the early 1980s after Hannes Alfven (a Swedish physicist) won a Nobel prize for his work with plasma.**

But back to the big three. Everything you see, taste, touch, or smell is a solid, a liquid, or a gas.

Solids include everything from pine trees to parachutes. Solid materials always have a definite shape and volume. This is because the particles in solids are much more tightly packed together than those in other forms of matter.

---

*And beyond these fundamental states of matter lies fermionic condensate and Bose-Einstein condensate. Definitely Sheldon Cooper territory!

**Alfven won his prize in 1970, but textbooks often lag years behind discoveries ... much to the dismay of teachers.

Liquids include everything from coffee to kerosene. Liquids have definite volumes, but they don't have definite shapes. The particles in liquids are less tightly packed together than the particles in a solid, but more tightly packed than those in a gas.

Gases include everything from the air we breathe to fuels like propane. A gas has no definite shape or volume. The particles in a gas are very loosely packed. They also tend to spread out, filling the area they are in.

It's important to note, however, that these categories are simply a convenient way of grouping matter. Some materials, like pitch (natural asphalt) strain the definitions. Although pitch looks like a solid, it's actually an extremely thick liquid.*

Matter can also change states.** Many materials change from one state to another when they are heated or cooled (or under pressure). When you heat a solid, it can turn into a liquid. When you heat a liquid, it can turn into a gas. When you cool a gas, it can condense into a liquid. When you cool a liquid, it can freeze into a solid.

Water is the most common example. At room temperature, water is a liquid. But if water gets cold enough, it will turn into a solid. Solid forms of water include ice, sleet, and hail. If water is heated enough, it can turn into a gas called steam (water vapor). But as steam cools, it turns back into liquid water.

Although solids, liquids, and gases are common on earth, *plasma* is the most common state of matter in space. Plasma is closely related to gases, but it is made of different particles. Like gas, plasma does not have a definite shape or a definite volume unless it's in a container. Unlike gas, plasma has the ability to respond

---

In 1930, a scientist poured pitch into a glass funnel and allowed it to begin dripping out. As of July 2014, only nine drops had fallen! The only thing slower may be Congress.

**although it may have to stop for a fruit inspection before entering California*

to electromagnetic fields, forming structures such as filaments, beams, and double layers.

The stars, the tails of comets, and the aurora borealis (northern lights) are all forms of plasma. Plasma not only forms many of the things we see in the night sky, but it also drifts through space between them.

Scientists are constantly researching the properties of plasma to discover new ways of producing energy. Although currently plasma technology is mostly used for neon signs and plasma TVs, many scientists believe that someday plasma may provide an endless source of energy for mankind.

Have Some Fun!

You'll need an Alka-Seltzer® tablet*, a clear cup, and water. Fill the cup half full of water. Drop the tablet into the water. Once the reaction begins, hold your hand over the cup for a moment. Now write down the states of matter you observed.

You can see that the tablet is a solid, the water is a liquid, and the reaction of the tablet with the water produced a gas. (By the way, the tablet didn't "melt," it dissolved. We'll talk about the difference in another chapter.)

Have Some MORE Fun!

Bonus Activity 1:
If you have a friend that works in the heating and air business, have him/her show you the monitoring equipment (gas leak detectors, pressure guages, etc.) associated with the profession. Ask for an explanation of how gases (like refrigerants) and liquids (like heating oil) are used to keep our homes comfortable.

*for the activity, not your heartburn

Bonus Activity 2:
For some great visuals, type "states of matter" into your search engine, then click on "videos." You'll find a number of presentations that explore this topic in much more depth. By the way, any visuals produced by kids often make up for in enthusiasm what they lack in professionalism! (That's one reason that I *love* being a teacher!)

National Standards

Here are the National Standards reflected in this chapter:

"Materials can exist in different states — solid, liquid, and gas. Some common materials, such as water, can be changed from one state to another by heating or cooling."
— **National Science Education Standards** (B1.C)

"In a solid, atoms are closely spaced and may vibrate in position but do not change relative locations. In a liquid, the molecules are constantly in contact with others. In a gas, they are widely spaced except when they happen to collide. The changes of state that occur with variations in temperature or pressure can be described and predicted."
— **Next Generation Science Standards** (PS1.A)

What You Learned

- Everything around you is made of matter, which can exist in different "states".

- Temperature or pressure may cause matter to change from one state to another.

- The most common states on Earth are solid, liquid, and gas.

- The most common state of matter in space is plasma.

Preview

Look at a sheet of paper. How many words can you use to describe its characteristics (color, size, shape, etc.)? Scientists call these characteristics "properties." Its properties are what make the paper different from all other materials.

Think about the properties of a pair of scissors. Use the scissors to cut the paper into several pieces. The properties of the paper and the scissors are what make this possible. In other words, you can't cut scissors with paper.

There are billions of objects and materials on earth. All of them have different properties. We can see something's size or color. We can feel its weight or its temperature. Properties help us describe things and determine how they can be used.

Essential Concepts

As we stated above, there are literally billions of objects in our world — from space shuttles to snails; from sandals to soup. All of these objects are different in many ways including size, shape, weight, color, and temperature. Scientists call these differences "properties." Properties are the unique characteristics that make one object or material different from another.

An object's properties can help determine how we use it. For example, a bowling ball is made of hard, heavy materials. These properties make it perfect for bowling. But the same properties would make it less than desirable for a game of volleyball!*

*Now THAT would be an extreme sport!

A material's properties also affect how it reacts with other materials. When you mix small grains of sugar in water, they dissolve. But if you mix grains of sand in the same amount of water, you only get a mess. Even though sand and sugar have some similarities, their properties are very different. (Ask anyone who has tried to eat a picnic on the beach!)

Properties are often used to sort groups of objects or materials. If you've ever driven by a recycling company, you may have seen powerful electromagnets separating shredded debris. The ferrous materials like iron and steel (except for stainless steel) stick to the electromagnet. Non-ferrous materials (like wood or plastic) do not.

Determining the properties of a material before you use it is very important. Never put a spoonful of white, granular material in your coffeee unless you know its properties. Sugar, salt, and some types of rat poison all look very similar! So how do scientists determine the properties of a material? The old "trial and error" method is not always the best choice.*

Scientists use special tools to measure the various properties of materials. Some are simple; some are very specialized. Rulers are used to measure the dimensions of an object. A balance can help determine its mass. Cups and cylinders measure the volume of a liquid. Meters can measure its flow. A thermometer measures temperature. A Geiger counter measures radioactivity. Each of these devices is designed to measure a very specific property.

Understanding the concept that materials have properties, and that these properties impact how we use them is very important. When you think about it, almost everything you do is affected by the properties of the objects and materials around you.

Otherwise we would quickly run out of scientists!

Have Some Fun!

This simple activity illustrates the basic concept of properties. (It also shows that many challenges have more than one solution.)

You'll need a small bag of Skittles®, a small bag of M&M's®, and a bowl. Open the bags and stir the Skittles® and M&M's® together in the bowl. Now choose a specific property and sort the candy into related piles based on the properties of each piece.* Once you're finished, repeat the activity using a different property.

As you can see, these materials have obvious properties like letters (M or S) and colors (green, yellow, orange, red, brown, etc.). But closer examination will also reveal more subtle properties like defective shapes, missing letters, core contents (chocolate or no chocolate), and so on.

Have Some MORE Fun!

Bonus Activity 1:
Simple writing activities are a great way to help your brain master basic concepts, so we'll be doing several of these throughout the book. For this activity, list pairs of objects or materials that have a major property in common, but are different in other ways. Examples include an ice cube and steam; a ping-pong ball and a golf ball; construction paper and tissue paper, etc.

Bonus Activity 2:
Peanuts are an example of a simple material with many properties. George Washington Carver (1864-1943) was an agricultural chemist who discovered over 300 uses for peanuts — most of which had nothing to do with food! Treat yourself to a book or watch a documentary about this amazing American.

Remember, good scientists don't eat their experiments!

National Standards

Here are the National Standards reflected in this chapter:

"Objects have many observable properties including size, weight, shape, color, temperature, and the ability to react with other substances. Those properties can be measured using tools such as rulers, balances, and thermometers."
— **National Science Education Standards** (B1.C)

"Matter can be described and classified by its observable properties. Different properties are suited to different purposes. Each pure substance has characteristic physical and chemical properties that can be used to identify it. Measurements of a variety of properties can be used to identify materials."
— **Next Generation Science Standards** (PS1.A)

What You Learned

• Matter has observable characteristics called "properties".

• Objects and materials can be described and sorted by their various properties.

• The properties of objects and materials make them suitable for different purposes.

• The properties of objects and materials can be measured using different types of tools.

Newton's Laws

Preview

This one is not for the faint of heart. Find a whistle. (Make sure it's a loud one.) Go to a place where there's some sort of crowd.* Wait until no one is paying attention, then blow your whistle loudly. Now smile so they know you're a harmless idiot, then walk away to reflect on what you observed.

When startled by an unexpected sound, most people will react in some way. The noise you made could be called an "action" and the response of the crowd a "reaction." While this was a sociological experiment rather than a physical one (we hope), the terminology is similar to Newton's Third Law of Motion. We'll explore all three of Newton's Laws in this chapter.

Essential Concepts

Objects on earth tend to follow consistent patterns of behavior, often referred to as "scientific laws."** In the late 1600s, an English scientist named Isaac Newton shared his ideas about how and why objects move.

Newton's descriptions about the position and motion of objects laid the foundation for modern mechanics. His findings are commonly known as "Newton's Laws."

Newton's First Law states that all objects resist change. Nothing can begin moving (or stop moving) unless some sort of force is applied. This resistance to change is called "inertia."

*somewhere **appropriate** ... a biker bar is probably not the best location for this
**Objects are much better at following laws than say Justin Bieber.

Because of inertia, an object will stay in place until some kind of force (a push or a pull) is applied to make it move. When your coffee cup is sitting on your desk, inertia will keep it there until an accidental push from your arm makes it fall off. Oops!

Inertia also means that once an object is moving, it takes some kind of force to make it change direction, change speed, or stop. When you throw a Frisbee®, inertia keeps it moving through the air. Without opposing forces like friction and gravity, the Frisbee® would just keep on flying away.

Newton's Second Law shows that mass (weight) and force (push or pull) affect an object's motion. Everything has mass, but large, heavy objects have more mass than small, light ones.*

Mass affects motion. Heavy objects are harder to move. But then, once they are moving, they are also harder to stop. It takes more force to move a dump truck than a skateboard. However, a moving truck is a lot harder to stop than a skateboard.

Force also affects motion [F=MA]. By pushing or pulling you can change an object's speed or direction. When you push a shopping cart, you can make it go faster or slower depending on how hard you push. You can also make it change directions by applying more force to one side of the handle or the other.

Newton's Third Law states that whenever a force is applied (an action), there is an equal force in the opposite direction (a reaction). Such forces always come in pairs. In other words, whenever you push or pull something, there is always a push or pull back in the other direction.

Imagine you are at an ice skating rink with your friend (who has never been skating before). You're trying to help him move around the rink by gently pushing him forward. However,

*Mass and weight aren't exactly the same, but we'll talk more about that later.

your friend suddenly decides that he'd rather do something less demanding (like skydiving), so he turns around and begins to push you back.

Regardless of who pushes whom, the two of you end up moving away from each other. The force (action) you applied is being opposed by the force that he applied (reaction).

Here's an even better example: When you sit on a chair, you are pushing down on the chair. But the chair pushes back up with an equal force. If it didn't, you'd end up on the floor.*

Remember, Newton's Third Law always involves an interaction between two things. As someone once said, "You can't touch something without being touched back."

Have Some Fun!

(Newton's Second Law) You'll need a small piece of carpet, a drinking straw, a golf ball, and a ping-pong ball. Set the golf ball on the carpet. Try to blow it off using the straw. Now repeat using the ping-pong ball. Notice that though the balls are roughly the same size and shape, their mass is very different. The golf ball barely moves, but the ping-pong ball rolls away easily! This clearly illustrates Newton's Second Law.

Have Some MORE Fun!

Bonus Activity 1:
(Newton's First Law) Research seat belts, air bags, crumple zones, and other safety devices that are designed to absorb or redirect force. Discover how each of these inventions save lives by applying the concept of inertia.

*or possibly the ceiling, although that's much less likely

Bonus Activity 2:
(Newton's Third Law) Research how rockets use the concept of action/reaction to get into space. NASA's website (www.nasa.gov) is a good place to start. You can also search the Internet for various videos on "propulsion."

National Standards

Here are the National Standards reflected in this chapter:

"The position and motion of objects can be changed by pushing or pulling. The size of the change is related to the strength of the push or pull."
  — **National Science Education Standards** (B2.C)

"Pushes and pulls can have different strengths and directions. Pushing or pulling on an object can change the speed or direction of motion and can start or stop it. The motion of an object is determined by the sum of the forces acting on it; if the total force on the object is not zero, its motion will change. The greater the mass of the object, the greater the force needed to achieve the same change in motion."
  — **Next Generation Science Standards** (PS2.A)

What You Learned

• The motion of objects follows scientific laws.

• Nothing can begin moving or stop moving unless a force is applied.

• Mass (weight) and force (push or pull) affect an object's motion.

• Whenever a force is applied (action), there is an equal force in the opposite direction (reaction).

Preview

Take a "power walk" through your home. Every time you pass an electrical device, turn it on and off. Notice how electricity produces different effects in different devices.*

Turn on a lamp, electricity produces **light**. Turn on an electric stove, electricity produces **heat**. Turn on a radio, electricity produces **sound**.** Turn on any device that has an electric motor, and electricity produces magnetic effects that will probably result in **motion**.

So how is this possible? It's all electricity, right? Actually, it's only one form of electricity. Let's take a closer look.

Essential Concepts

Electricity comes in different forms. The three most common forms of electricity are static electricity, direct current, and alternating current.

Static electricity is that stuff that you learned to fear as a kid. It's produced by friction between certain kinds of materials.*** When your sneaky kid sister walked across shag carpeting in wool socks, then snuck up behind you and touched the tip of your ear ... yeah, that was static electricity.

---

*Make a detailed list if your name is Adrian Monk.

**Unless, of course, it's set to your teenager's favorite station ... then less favorable terms come to mind.

***including siblings

Bathroom rugs and metal doornobs can do the trick, too. If it's dark, you can even see the electricity flow from your hand to the metal in the form of a bright spark. Ouch!

Lightning is an even more dramatic display of static electricity. The turbulence in thunderstorms creates static charges that build up until they're released as bolts of lightning. (Just don't try Ben Franklin's dangerous stunt. An attempt to replicate Ben's kite trick killed Russian scientist Georg Richmann in 1753.)

Another form of electricity is **direct current**. This is the form most commonly associated with batteries. Electricity flows from the battery to the load, then back again in a simple loop. For example, when you turn on a flashlight, you're using direct current to light up the bulb.

In 1882, Thomas Edison used direct current to light several homes near his workshop. This was America's first electrical distribution system.*

Alternating current is the form of electicity that powers most homes and offices. Alternating current flows in rapid back-and-forth cycles, making it easier to transfer across long distances.

In 1892, Nikola Tesla ran alternating current from Niagara Falls to Buffalo, New York. This was America's first *long-distance* electrical distribution system.**

Both direct current and alternating current are usually produced by spinning a turbine attached to a generator. These turbines are driven by wind, water, or the steam produced from coal, natural gas, or nuclear reactions.

---

*It also began the "war of currents" between Edison and Tesla, which eventually led to the electrocution of Topsy the elephant ... but that's another story.

**Take that, Mr. Edison!

Once the electricity is produced, it's transferred through electrical transmission lines to the point where it will be used. It powers our lights, heaters, air conditioners, radios, fans, computers, appliances ... and cappuccino machines!

Have Some Fun!

Alternating current can be dangerous, but low-voltage direct current is relatively safe. This low-voltage circuit shows how electricity flows in a loop from a battery through a bulb, then back to the battery again. You'll need a D-cell battery, two feet of 20 gauge wire, a simple flashlight bulb, and electrical tape.

First, cut the wire into two 12-inch pieces. Strip the insulation off all four ends. Now wrap the end of wire #1 around the bulb's threads, then tape the other end to the negative end of the battery. Next, tape one end of wire #2 to the positive end of the battery.

Ready? Carefully touch the other end of wire #2 to the contact on bulb's base. This will complete the circuit, making the bulb light up.*

Have Some MORE Fun!

Bonus Activity 1:
Check to see that you've mastered the concepts in this chapter by making a list of the electrical devices you have in your home. Sort these into four categories based on each device's primary purpose: light, heat, sound, or motion.

Note that some of these devices may produce secondary effects. For example, a lamp is primarily for light ... but it can produce a fair amount of heat, too!

*If the baby's not asleep, shout "voila!" (French for "wah lah!")

Bonus Activity 2:
If you're up for a challenge, go "off grid" for a day. You may need to walk or bike to work*; skip the heating or air conditioning; do without electronic devices and appliances**; and use candles or lanterns to light your house after dark.

Try this for 24 hours, and you'll get a glimpse of the conditions that nearly a quarter of the world's population faces every day.

National Standards

Here are the National Standards reflected in this chapter:

"Electricity in circuits can produce light, heat, sound, and magnetic effects. Electrical circuits require a complete loop through which an electrical current can pass."
— **National Science Education Standards** (B3.C)

"Energy can be transferred from place to place by electrical currents, which can then be used locally to produce motion, sound, heat, or light."
— **Next Generation Science Standards** (PS4.B)

What You Learned

- The three basic forms of electricity are static electricity, direct current, and alternating current.

- Electricity can be used to produce light, heat, sound, and magnetic effects that can cause motion.

- Electricity is usually produced by spinning a turbine attached to a generator. Turbines can be driven by wind, water, or steam.

*assuming you woke up without the alarm on your clock radio
**no phones, computers, recorded music, or (gasp!) microwave popcorn

Preview

Place a small toy on the right edge of a large table. Darken the room, then set a flashlight at the front of the table so that it is aimed at the toy. Is the light hitting the toy? (*Yes, of course it is!*) Now move the toy to the left edge of the table, but keep the flashlight the same. Is the light hitting the toy now? (*No, it's not.*) Why not? (*Light travels in a straight line.*) Leave everything the same, but use a mirror to reflect the light onto the toy. Now is light hitting the toy? (*Yes, because the mirror is redirecting the light into a new path.*) This serves to introduce some of the basic properties of light we'll explore in this chapter.

Essential Concepts

We live in a world filled with light.* Some sources of light (like the sun, glowworms, fireflies, and some fungi) are natural. Other sources of light (like lamps, strobes, welding arcs, and lasers) are artificial.

Light usually travels in a straight line. But when light strikes an object, it can bounce off. Light that bounces off is ***reflected***. Light that bends is ***refracted***. And light that is soaked up is ***absorbed***. Let's look closer at each of these.

In order for us to see any object, light must be ***reflected*** back from it (unless the object itself gives off light). Reflected light can also bounce back images. Shiny materials like water, chrome, or glass often reflect nearby objects. One beautiful example is snow-capped mountains reflecting in a still mountain lake.

except at night ... or if you're a bat

Mirrors make great reflectors. Images in mirrors are reflected right-side up, but are reversed front to back. (Reflections in mirrors are not left to right as many assume).

This type of reflected light is very useful. Imagine trying to fix your hair or brush your teeth without the reflection of a mirror! Reflected light can also help a driver backing up a truck, a dentist checking your teeth, or a clerk watching the aisles of a store.

Refracted light is "bent." Refracted light can magnify an image. The curved surface of a lens can refract light, making an object appear bigger or smaller.* This application of refracted light is used in many tools, including cameras, telescopes, microscopes, and lasers. Refracted light helps many people see better. Reading glasses and contacts use a special type of refractive lens.

Refracted light can also make colors appear. If the angle is just right, raindrops can refract sunlight into its basic colors producing a rainbow. Crystals placed in a window can refract sunlight to make tiny rainbows. Laser shows use complex, high-tech optical components to refract light, creating colorful moving beams.

Refracted light can even create illusions. Place a pencil in a glass of water. Look at the glass from the side, and refraction will make the pencil look bent or broken.** Primitive hunters had to learn how to compensate for the refraction of light when spearfishing, or go home hungry.

What about *absorbed* light? Objects with dark, dull colors absorb sunlight. This can change light into heat, making an object hot. But objects with light, shiny colors *reflect* light. When an object does not absorb sunlight, it stays much cooler. That's why most summer clothing is white or some light color. (You can prove this by wearing a black t-shirt to a ballgame on a bright, sunny day!)

Although, for some reason, I always appear to look bigger.

**and also wet*

Light absorption also affects the perceived color of an object. Natural sunlight contains all the colors of light, but only the colors that are not absorbed are seen. For example, growing grass absorbs all colors except green. The green light is reflected, making grass look green.

Some newer technologies use absorbed light, too. Solar panels absorb sunlight to warm water or generate electricity. (I once got second degree burns from underestimating how fast my home-made solar panel could heat water on a cold winter day!)

Have Some Fun!

Share this one with some kids ... it's cool! You'll need a clear glass jar, a small hand mirror, a flashlight with a bright narrow beam, and water. Place the mirror in the jar with the bottom touching the side closest to you and the top tilted back. Darken the room, the place the flashlight against the jar and shine it at the mirror. Observe what happens. Now fill the jar with water and repeat the previous step. Observe what happens.

In Step 1, you'll see the light reflect and appear on the ceiling. But in Step 2, the light will reflect *and* refract. This will usually make faint colors appear at the edge of the light where it's shining on the ceiling.

Have Some MORE Fun!

Bonus Activity 1:
Play the "Reflection Detection" game. In five minutes, list all the items you can think of that use mirrors in some way. These can be common items like household mirrors — but can also include more unusual types of mirrors like those found in flashlights, telescopes, or on cars. Do this alone or compete with a partner. When time is up, use the Internet to find more.

Bonus Activity 2:
Play "Refraction Action." This game is similar to "Reflection Detection," but this time you list various objects that bend light in some way. (Think about devices that use lenses, or natural refractors like raindrops, or even fun house mirrors.)

National Standards

Here are the National Standards reflected in this chapter:

"Light travels in a straight line until it strikes an object. Light can be reflected by a mirror, refracted by a lens, or absorbed by the object."
— **National Science Education Standards** (B3.A)

"Objects can be seen if light is available to illuminate them or if they give off their own light. The path that light travels can be traced as straight lines, except at surfaces between different transparent materials where the light path bends. When light shines on an object, it is reflected, absorbed, or transmitted through the object, depending on the material. Mirrors can be used to redirect a light beam."
— **Next Generation Science Standards** (PS3.B)

What You Learned

• Light sources can be natural or artificial.

• Light travels in a straight line until it strikes an object.

• Light can be reflected by shiny materials (like a mirror).

• Light can be refracted by curved surfaces (like lenses).

• Light can be absorbed, producing heat.

Preview

Place your palms together and rub them back and forth rapidly. Continue this action until your hands get hot. Now wave your hands around in the air, allowing them to cool back down.*

The activity you just did was a science experiment involving heat production. In this chapter, we'll explore three different ways that heat can be produced. Some are simple physical actions (like the experiment you just did). Other ways of producing heat involve chemical actions or mixing things together.

Essential Concepts

Heat is an important form of energy. Heat can come from either natural sources or artificial sources. Natural heat sources have been around since the world began. They include the sun, lightning, and fire. Artificial heat comes from devices made by people. Examples include dryers, curling irons, and furnaces.**

The most common forms of heat come from physical actions or chemical reactions. A *physical* action produces heat without changing a substance. A *chemical* reaction changes the substance into a different substance.

Friction is a *physical* action. Friction produces heat when two objects rub together, or an object rubs against another surface. When this rubbing produces friction, energy is released as heat. The greater the friction, the greater the heat.

*This should amuse your pets.
**... and Disney's Steampunk Fire-Breathing Dragon!

31

Since it's a physical action, friction doesn't change a substance. As you saw in the Preview, if you rub your hands together rapidly, friction makes your hands hot ... but they are still your hands. Once the friction stops, your hands just get cooler.

By contrast, burning is a **chemical** reaction. It takes just the right mixure of fuel, air, and a heat source to start something burning.* When you burn something, energy is released as heat. The longer something burns, the more heat is released.

Since it's a chemical reaction, burning changes a substance. When someone builds a campfire, the burning logs release a lot of heat. But when the fire finally burns out, the ashes don't turn back into wood. The process has produced a different substance.

Some chemical reactions are very slow. Rotting and rusting are good examples of slow chemical reactions that release heat.

Other chemical reactions happen very fast. Mixing certain substances together may cause a rapid reaction. For example, activating a hand warmer mixes special substances that produce instant heat. This heat lasts until the reaction is complete.

You might be surprised that eating is a chemical reaction, too! Food and stomach acids mix together, releasing heat energy to power your body. So in a sense, one cause of obesity is over ingestion of non-optimal chemicals. In other words, we eat too much of the wrong stuff!**

Whether the heat comes from natural or artificial sources, heat is a form of energy. And like other forms of energy, heat can move from one place to another.

A common way for heat energy to move is through "conduction." Conduction can transfer heat from one object to another. If you

---

*Ask any frustrated Boy Scout holding two sticks.
**Thank you, Ben and Jerry!

put a metal spoon in a cup of hot coffee, the spoon will get hot. Conduction moves heat from the coffee into the spoon.

Here's another example. Touch a metal desk and it often feels a little bit cold. That's conduction moving heat away from your fingers and into the metal.*

Have Some Fun!

You'll need a pencil, a plastic spoon, a metal spoon, a tall glass, hot water, butter, and paper towel. Spread a small pat of butter on the end of the pencil, the handle of the plastic spoon, and the handle of the metal spoon. Place the glass on the paper towel, then set the pencil and the spoons in the glass, buttered end up. Now pour hot water into the glass. Monitor to see which pat of butter melts off first.

This activity demonstrates the concept of conduction. The butter should fall off the handle of the metal spoon first. Why? Because metal is a better conductor of heat than wood or plastic.

Have Some MORE Fun!

Bonus Activity 1:
This activity is a bit more advanced. Place a thermometer in a half cup of water. Crush up some road salt de-icer (calcium chloride) and add a tablespoon full to the water. Observe the temperature rise.

This clearly illustrates the difference between physical and chemical change. Even though the calcium chloride seems to disappear, it remains the same substance. (If you let the water evaporate, the calcium chloride will still be there.)

also demonstrated by warm back vs. cold feet sleeping arrangements

Bonus Activity 2:
Contact a "waste management services" company (or your city maintenance department) to find out the location of the nearest commerical composting facility. Take a mini-field trip and ask an employee to show you how decomposing compost produces heat.

National Standards

Here are the National Standards reflected in this chapter:

"Heat can be produced in many ways, such as burning, rubbing, or mixing one substance with another. Heat can move from one object to another by conduction."
    — **National Science Education Standards** (B3.B)

"Heating or cooling a substance may cause changes that can be observed. Sometimes these changes are reversible, and sometimes they are not. The term 'heat' ... refers to the transfer of thermal energy from one object to another."
    — **Next Generation Science Standards** (PS1.B) (PS3.A)

What You Learned

- Heat sources can be natural or artificial.

- Physical actions like friction can produce heat.

- Physical actions do not change a substance.

- Chemical actions like burning can produce heat.

- Chemical actions change a substance into a different substance.

- Mixing substances together can produce heat.

- Heat can move between objects through conduction.

Preview

You'll need some duct tape*, six toothpicks, six paperclips, a small box, and a magnet. Wrap the toothpicks in a piece of duct tape so that they can't be seen. Do the same thing with the paperclips. Place the two tiny bundles in the box and shake it around.

Take the bundles out of the box and place them on the table. Without using the magnet, try to determine which bundle is which. Now use the magnet to do the same thing. See how much more efficient that is? Sorting materials is just one use for magnetism. You'll discover a lot more in this chapter.

Essential Concepts

One sunny afternoon about 3,000 years ago, an elderly shepherd named Magnes sat down on a large rock to take a rest. Suddenly, the nails in his shoes and the iron tip of his staff became stuck to the rock. Thus, the first magnet was discovered.

Of course, it's impossible to know if this ancient legend is true. However, there are surviving descriptions of magnets (lodestones) and their properties from Greece, India, and China that date back at least 2,500 years.

In addition to discovering that these rare stones would attract iron, the ancients found that if one of them was hung from a string,** it would always point in the same direction! They were amazed at this invisible force. The clever ways that magnets are used today grew out of those early discoveries.

*a "must have" tool for the budget-minded scientist

**the stones, not the ancients

There are three primary types of magnets — temporary magnets, permanent magnets, and electromagnets.

Some types of iron are easily magnetized. Rub a magnet against a piece of this iron, and you can make a *temporary* magnet. But this type of magnet soon loses its power.*

Permanent magnets are magnets that are always working. Natural magnets, like lodestone, are the most common. But permanent magnets can also be man-made.

Electromagnets are activated by the flow of electricity. These "on demand" magnets can be regulated by the flick of a switch.

Magnets are surrounded by fields of force, often represented by lines. In a drawing, the closer the lines, the stronger the magnetic force. The strongest areas of magnetic force are called the "poles." All magnets have a north pole and a south pole. The opposite poles of magnets (north and south) will pull toward or "attract" each other. The poles that are the same (north and north, or south and south) will push away or "repel" each other.

Some materials (like iron, nickel, and many types of steel) are said to be magnetic. These materials are strongly attracted by magnets. Other materials (like wood, plastic, or metals like aluminum or copper) are not magnetic. This means they are not attracted by magnets.

The properties of a magnet make it useful for many things. A magnet can be used to indicate direction. The magnetic needle of a compass will always point north. Magnetism can also hold things in place. You probably have at least one refrigerator magnet holding up a note or a picture.** And as we discussed earlier, magnets can also help us sort things. Huge electromagnets help separate ferrous metals from non-ferrous materials.

*much like teen pop stars
**or a button that says, "To err is human; to arrh is pirate!"

Magnetism also makes work easier. Magnets are an integral part of the huge electric generators used in power plants to produce electricity. Magnets inside electric motors help power appliances and tools. Magnetism can also store information. Devices like computers and credit cards can use magnetism to store data.

Magnetism can even be used for fun. There are hundreds of magnetic toys and building sets available for tinkering tots*. And although they're perfectly safe around today's computers,** just don't get one too close to a vintage floppy drive!

Have Some Fun!

This is one of the few activities in the book that may require purchased supplies. You'll need a sheet of paper, a bar magnet (check your local craft store), and iron filings or steel shavings. (Buy these online or beg some from a local machine shop.)

Set the magnet on the table. Cover it with the sheet of paper. Now slowly sprinkle the filings or shavings over the magnet. If you do this correctly, you should be able to see the lines of force from the magnetic field generated by the magnet.

Have Some MORE Fun!

Bonus Activity 1:
This is similar to the "Reflection Detection" game (page 29). In five minutes, list all the items you can think of that use magnets in some way. These can be houshold items (like refrigerator magnets or the part of an electric can opener that holds the lids), or more unusual magnets (like those in car generators, compasses, and the magnetic sweepers roofers use). Do this alone or compete with a partner. When time is up, use the Internet to find more.

*when they can pry them away from their parents
**the magnets, not the tots

Bonus Activity 2:
Research the history of magnet science. Focus on famous people who first learned about magnets and what magnets can do. This obscure topic has a lot of interesting information to explore.

National Standards

Here are the National Standards reflected in this chapter:

"Magnets attract and repel each other and certain kinds of materials."
— **National Science Education Standards** (B3.D)

"Magnets or electric currents cause magnetic fields. Electric and magnetic forces between a pair of objects do not require that the objects be in contact. (These) forces can be attractive or repulsive, and their sizes depend on the magnitudes of the charges, currents, or magnetic strengths involved and on the distances between the interacting objects."
— **Next Generation Science Standards** (PS2.B)

What You Learned

• Magnets and their properties have been explored since ancient times.

• There are three basic types of magnets — temporary, magnets, permanent magnets, and electromagnets

• Areas of strongest force on a magnet are called poles. Opposite poles attract; like poles repel.

• The properties of magnetic fields make magnets useful in many different ways.

Sound

Preview

In science, a "wave" is disturbance that travels through matter or space accompanied by a transfer of energy. **Mechanical** waves include seismic waves, sound waves, and the waves in fluids. **Electromagnetic** waves include radio waves, microwaves, infrared radiation, visible light, ultraviolet radiation, x-rays, and gamma rays.

Waves have energy, and they can transfer energy when they interact with matter. There are hundreds of books written about the various waves,* so for this chapter, we'll just focus on one type of wave (sound) to better understand some basic concepts.

Essential Concepts

Sound is a form of energy. It's produced by rapid back and forth movements called vibrations. Although a vibration can travel through a solid, liquid, or gas, most sounds we hear travel through the air.

When an object moves, it causes the air particles around it to vibrate rapidly. As they vibrate, they bump into the air particles next to them, causing these particles to vibrate, too. Particles continue bumping into other particles, carrying the vibration along.** This movement is called a sound wave.

Sound waves travel through the air around us constantly. So what is it that makes these sounds sound different?

*not to mention the movie **Point Break**

**somewhat like the movement of disco dancers in the 70s

Imagine dropping a stone into a pool of water. The impact makes waves that quickly expand outward. But if you drop a different stone, the waves will be closer together or farther apart. The pattern you see will change.

Sound waves work in a similar fashion. Different vibrations create different sounds, changing what you hear. Fast vibrations make sound waves that are closer together. Slow vibrations make sound waves that are farther apart.

The distance between the peaks of these waves is called the *wavelength*. In simple terms, shorter (closer) wavelengths make higher sounds, while longer (farther apart) wavelengths make lower sounds.

Wavelength is just one term scientists use to describe sound waves. Other common terms include frequency and amplitude. *Frequency* has to do with how fast the waves are coming (think speed). *Amplitude* means how much waves vary in height.

Here's an interesting application of these concepts. In the early days of radio, stations were AM or "amplitude modulated." In AM radio, information (speech, music, etc.) is transmitted by varying the height of the sound waves.

But AM had a major drawback for the military during combat. Explosions also affect the height of sound waves!* In certain situations, this made communications difficult or impossible. So during WWII, the military switched to the newer FM signals. FM ("frequency modulated") stations transmit information by changing wavelength and frequency instead of height. Thus FM signals are much less susceptible to outside interference like thunderstorms or explosions.**

Humans have learned how to create many complex sounds

*enough to seriously damage your hearing
**or the curious creatures that inhabit AM talk radio

that are used in a myriad of ways. In addition to communication, sounds can be used to create music.

Music is based on the careful arrangement of different sounds.* Singers tighten or relax their throats to change the sound. Guitar players use their fingers to make strings shorter or longer, changing the sound. Clarinet players open and close holes, letting more or less air through and changing the sound.

Sounds are even used in defense and medicine. Submarines use sonar (a special type of low sound) to find other submarines or locate things on the ocean floor. A doctor can use ultra-sound (high-frequency sound waves) to examine important features of an unborn baby.**

Have Some Fun!

You'll need four identical clear glasses, a ruler or measuring tape, a wooden pencil, and water. Pour one inch of water into Glass 1, two inches into Glass 2, three inches into Glass 3, and four inches into Glass 4. Now lightly tap the pencil against each glass in turn to see how the sound changes. Less water in the glass means that it vibrates slower, producing a lower sound. More water means it vibrates faster, producing a higher sound. With practice, you can even play a simple tune!

Have Some MORE Fun!

Bonus Activity 1:
Research how specific animals use sound to communicate. Interesting examples include dolphins, elephants, whales, and various birds. Think about the similarities and differences in these sounds and what it takes to produce them.

with the possible exception of Rap

**like whether or not it's wearing cleats as its mother claims*

Bonus Activity 2:
Check to see if your local radio or TV station gives tours.*
Ask the engineer to show you some of the equipment used to
measure sound. Have him/her demonstrate its use, and explain
why monitoring and measuring sound is important.

National Standards

Here are the National Standards reflected in this chapter:

*"Sound is produced by vibrating objects. Sound can be varied by
changing the rate of vibration. Waves (including sound waves, seismic
waves, waves on water, and light waves) have energy and can transfer
energy when they interact with matter ... Electromagnetic waves
include radio waves, microwaves, infrared radiation, visible light,
ultraviolet radiation, x-rays, and gamma rays."*
— **National Science Education Standards** (B2.D) (B6.A) (B6.B)

*"Sound can make matter vibrate, and vibrating matter can make
sound. Waves of the same type can differ in amplitude (height) and
wavelength (spacing). A simple wave has a repeating pattern with a
specific wavelength, frequency, and amplitude."*
— **Next Generation Science Standards** (PS4.A)

What You Learned

• Waves can transfer energy when they interact with matter.

• Sound is a type of wave produced when objects vibrate.

• Changing the shape of a sound wave changes the sound.

• Sound waves can travel through solids, liquids, and gases.

*or see if you can tag along with a school group

Life Science

"Half of modern drugs could well be thrown out of the window ... except that the birds might eat them."

– Martin H. Fischer

Structure & Function

Preview

Make a list of various kinds of buildings you've seen. Now think about the differences in their designs. For example, what are some ways that the structure of an automotive repair shop is different from a restaurant? Focus on how the structure of the building relates to its function. (*Repair shops have large garage doors, but restaurants don't. Why? Repair shops need to move cars inside, but restaurants only need people-size doors.*)*

In this book, you'll discover that living things have structures, too. These structures are designed to serve different functions in the organism's survival, behavior, growth, and reproduction.

Essential Concepts

Every living thing has certain parts that are made in certain ways (*structure*) so that it can do certain kinds of jobs (*function*). This is true for both plants and animals. The best way to gain a clearer understanding of this concept is to look at several examples.

If you've ever snorkled off the California coast, you may have seen forests of giant kelp. This plant has special air bladders that float, lifting the kelp's leaves toward the surface so that they can absorb energy from the sun.**

In the American Southwest, you'll find a very different kind of plant. The barrel cactus has a spongy inside that helps it store rainwater for long periods of time. Barrel cacti are also covered with long, sharp spines that protect them from being eaten.

*although "all you can eat" buffets may soon have to reconsider this
**and making it easier for the plant to harass surfers

Trees often have very specialized structures. The bald cypress has root projections called "knees" that stick up above the water to absorb oxygen for the roots. Banyan trees have "prop roots" that grow down from limbs, helping them spread over a wide area. (The "courthouse banyan" in Lahaina, Hawaii covers almost an entire city block!)

Similar creatures often use structure in very different ways. A tuna has a streamlined shape that helps it swim rapidly to avoid being eaten by a predator. But a rockfish uses an entirely different approach — it lies completely still, using its unique coloring to keep it hidden. Or look at birds. Eagles have strong, powerful wings that help them fly high and far in order to spot a potential meal. Penguins also have strong wings, but their wings are designed to help them swim rapidly underwater.

The animal world is filled with examples of structure and function. Female mosquitoes have piercing mouthparts that let them suck the blood they need to develop and lay eggs. Dart frogs are poisonous, but their bright-colored skin warns hungry predators that eating them is a bad idea. Badgers have strong, sharp claws that help them dig burrows for a safe place to raise their young. Cheetahs have long, muscular legs that help them run faster, making it easier to catch their prey.

Just like plants and animals, humans have different structures that serve different functions, too. For example, movement depends on the structure of your body.* Imagine trying to feed yourself without elbows — or running without knees! And a human's flexible fingers and thumbs can perform a variety of tasks from typing to holding bottles to grasping someone's hand.

Vision depends on eye structure. Like most predators, humans have eyes on the front of their heads that look straight ahead. Prey animals like rabbits, however, have eyes on the sides of their heads, allowing them to monitor a larger area without moving.

*Mine has a lot in common with the rockfish.

Even communication depends on structure. Humans use their mouth structure (lips, tongue, and other speech organs) to form the sounds of words. Other mammals, like dolphins, use specific sounds to communicate.* These sounds are always directly related to the creature's structure.

Strong wings, sharp claws, and flexible fingers are all examples of the relationship between structure and function. Without the correct match between structure and function, an organism chances of survival are greatly diminished.**

Have Some Fun!

You'll need two paper cups, water, food coloring (red and blue), a sharp knife, and a fresh white carnation. Fill the two paper cups with water. Add red food coloring to Cup A, and blue food coloring to Cup B. Split the stem of the carnation halfway up from the bottom. Set the cups next to each other, then place the end of a stem half in each cup. Prop the flower carefully so it doesn't fall over, and allow it to sit and soak overnight.

The stem halves will absorb water from different cups, staining one part of the flower red and the other blue! This demonstrates both the structure and the function of a flower stem.

Have Some MORE Fun!

Bonus Activity 1:
Compare water mammals (dolphins, seals, whales) to land mammals (rabbits, cows, squirrels). List ways these creatures are similar and different, then think about how this relates to structure and function.

except, apparently, with dolphin scientists

** *This may account for reduced populations of Texas armadillos, whose structure is entirely too similar to the modern speed bump.*

Bonus Activity 2:
Research various types of traveling seeds that are wind-borne, water-borne, or that "hitchhike." (Maple seeds, coconuts, and cockleburs are good examples.) Think about how the unique structure of these seeds contributes to their dispersal and subsequent survival.

National Standards

Here are the National Standards reflected in this chapter:

"Each plant or animal has different structures that serve different functions in growth, survival, and reproduction. For example, humans have distinct body structures for walking, holding, seeing, and talking."
— **National Science Education Standards** (C1.B)

"Plants and animals have both internal and external structures that serve various functions in growth, survival, behavior, and reproduction."
— **Next Generation Science Standards** (LS1.A)

What You Learned

• All living things have different parts (structures).

• Different structures serve different purposes (functions).

• An organism's structure affects how it survives, behaves, grows, and reproduces.

Basic Needs

Preview

We're *not* going to start this chapter by taking two perfectly innocent plants, and placing one in the sunlight and the other in the closet until one (or possibly both) die. I'm sure there's a plant group similar to PETA that would me write angry letters. Instead, we'll take a tip from reality TV shows* that are based on the premise of being stranded somewhere with limited resources.

Imagine you're on a sinking ship, and you only have time to remove one suitcase full of supplies before it goes down.** Make a list of what you think you'd need if you were stranded on a deserted island for months. Now review your list and think about the difference between "needs" (food, water, etc.) and "wants" (tanning lotion, neck pillow, iPod, etc.).

Essential Concepts

All living things need certain things in order to survive. These are called *basic needs*. For example, air is a basic need. Air is made of gases like nitrogen, oxygen, and carbon dioxide. A moving layer of air surrounds the earth, and except for some kinds of bacteria, all life on earth needs air in order to survive.

Water is another basic need. Over seventy percent of Earth's surface is covered with water. Not only do we drink water and wash in water — most living things are made from a high percentage of water. More than half the human body is water, and an adult jellyfish can be almost all water!

*not to be confused with actual reality
**the ship, not the suitcase

49

Food is another basic need. There are many kinds of food, from plants eaten by animals to soil nutrients that are "food" for plants. Living things get food in many different ways. But all living things need some form of food in order to survive.

Light is also a basic need. Sunlight helps plants absorb nutrients and convert light energy to food energy. Although too much sun can be harmful,* humans get much of the vitamin D they need from exposure to sunlight.

An organism's environment must supply all its basic needs, but there are many different kinds of environments. An environment can be very hot or very cold, very wet or very dry, very light or very dark — and everything in between. There are creatures that can survive in almost every kind of environment on Earth. Let's look at a few examples:

Many unique lizards thrive in the very hot environment of the tropics. The Komodo dragon can reach a length of over ten feet and weigh over 300 pounds. By contrast, a basilisk is about three inches long, and is so light it can run for several feet across the surface of a lake or pond. (Fortunately, it can also swim.)

The extremely cold temperatures of the Arctic would spell a quick end for most creatures. But the Arctic hare's fur insulates it so well that it can live for several days at temperatures far below freezing just on its stored body fat.**

The aquatic enviroment of the ocean poses many challenges. Yet manatees comfortably cruise the shallows of the Keys, while dragonfish lurk at depths so great it would crush a submarine.

Deserts are another extreme environment. But creatures many creatures, like gerbils, have adapted so well that they need very little water to survive and thrive.

*and the beef jerky look is definitely out of style
**don't try this at home

50

In any ecosystem, organisms may compete with each other for food, water, and other basic needs. When these resources are limited, or when the environment changes, creatures must move, adapt, or die.

Sometimes, mans' actions change environments. Deforestation in East Africa has almost eliminated the natural habitat of gorillas. Agricultural runoff threatens the Everglades. And it's impossible to calculate the full extent of damage to the ecosystem from accidents like the *Exxon Valdez* and *Deepwater Horizon* oil spills.* Since a healthy environment is vital in meeting mankind's basic needs, taking care of it is just good sense!

Have Some Fun!

So *now* we'll kill some plants! You'll need a food storage bag, two small plants (like tomato seedlings), and water. Place one plant in a moderately sunny location, and water it well. This plant will be the "control" for the experiment. Shake all the soil off the roots of the other plant. Seal it in the food storage bag, then place the bag in a very dark location. Wait three days, then compare the two plants. The plant whose needs were met (air, water, sunlight, nutrients) should be healthy and strong. The plant whose needs were not met will be dead or dying.

Have Some MORE Fun!

Bonus Activity 1:
To demonstrate how plants need sunlight, place a small board on a patch of grass.** Wait about a week, then lift the board to see how the grass has changed. Think about what basic needs were not being met.

although highly-paid corporate attorneys continue to try
**your own, not your neighbor's*

Bonus Activity 2:
Watch a video about a region where human basic needs are not being met — Ethiopia, Honduras, Appalachia, etc. Research possible reasons for the problems and possible solutions.

National Standards

Here are the National Standards reflected in this chapter:

"Organisms have basic needs ... Organisms can survive only in environments in which their needs can be met. The world has many different environments, and distinct environments support the life of different types of organisms."
 — **National Science Education Standards** (C1.A)

"Plants depend on water and light to grow. Food provides animals with the materials they need for body repair and growth and the energy they need to maintain body warmth and for motion. In any ecosystem, organisms and populations with similar requirements for food, water, oxygen, or other resources may compete with each other for limited resources, access to which consequently constrains their growth and reproduction."
 — **Next Generation Science Standards** (LS1.C) (LS2.A)

What You Learned

• All organisms have basic needs.

• Basic needs may include air, water, food, and light.

• Earth has many different environments which support many different types of life.*

• Organisms can only survive when environments support their basic needs.

*many of which can be seen on late night TV

Life Cycles

Preview

Every morning, people all over America make their beds.* They smooth the sheets, pull up the covers, then add the pillows. At night, they pull down the covers and sheets and climb in the bed to sleep. But the next morning, they start the process all over again. This repetitive process is called a "cycle."

Our lives have cycles, too. Have you ever seen a picture of an elderly friend or relative when that person was still a baby? Think about what they looked like then as opposed to the way they look now. Being born, growing into an adult, having children, and eventually dying is all part of the human life cycle.

Essential Concepts

All living things have life cycles — from plankton, to peas, to penguins, to people. These life cycles usually include four major stages. First, something is born. Over time, it grows into an adult. Once it is an adult, it may reproduce, helping ensure that its species will continue. Eventually, it will die.

Although life cycles usually have four stages, the details can vary enormously between insects, plants, birds, and mammals — not to mention differences within these groups. (With over 5,000 known species of mammals, there's a lot of variation!)

Most plants start as seeds. When conditions are right, seeds begin to sprout. Sprouting seeds grow into adult plants. When plants are grown, they produce more seeds. These seeds fall to the ground to start the life cycle over again.

except for teenagers, frat boys, and bachelors

53

Most insects and birds start their life cycle as eggs. Bird eggs hatch into baby birds, and baby birds grow into adult birds. When an adult female bird lays eggs, the life cycle will begin over again.

Most mammals (including humans) have babies. These babies will eventually grow into adults.* When adult mammals reproduce, a baby is born. With this birth, the mammal's life cycle starts over again.

It's important to note that mature living things are phsyically a lot like their parents. Puppies always look like dogs, not cats. Chicks will always look like chickens, not ducks. A calf always looks like a cow, not a horse.

The same is true for plants. An acorn from an oak tree will never grow into a pine tree. Tomato plants will always produce tomatoes, not squash. Wheat seeds always produce wheat, not rice or corn.

But even though organisms share many characteristics with their parents, every living thing is still unique.* Even if you have the same hair, eye color, facial features, and physical build as your parents (or a twin), you are still uniquely you!

Here's an interesting example: Which do you think is a more positive identifier in a criminal investigation ... fingerprints or DNA evidence?

In 2009, Berlin police were investigating a multi-millon dollar jewel heist. They found DNA evidence "in a drop of sweat on a latex glove discarded next to a rope ladder." This evidence led them to identical twins. However, a German court had to let them go because "we can deduce that at least one of the brothers took part in the crime, but [based on the available evidence] it has not been possible to determine which one."

*or at least a reasonable facsimile thereof
**We'll talk more about this in the chapter on Heredity.

Had police been able to gather fingerprints, however, the outcome would have been very different. Even though the fingerprints of idential twins are extremely similar, the patterns are unique for each individual.

And this is not the only case where fingerprints would have helped with a conviction. A paternity trial in Houston in 2005 and a drug-smuggling case in Malaysia in 2009 ran into similar problems with twins.

So, in spite of what you've seen on TV crime shows, the surprising answer is that fingerprints are often more helpful than DNA!

Have Some Fun!

Here's your chance to see the beginnings of a life cycle in action. You'll need alfalfa seeds for sprouting (available at any natural foods store), a clear glass jar, a tablespoon, a rubber band, and a piece of pantyhose. Place two tablespoons of seeds in the glass jar. Fill the jar half full of water and let the seeds soak overnight.

The next day, attach a layer of pantyhose to the jar opening with the rubber band. Invert the jar and drain off all the water. Now lay the jar on its side in a warm place. Rinse and drain the seeds once each day until they begin to sprout — usually three or four days. This activity demonstrates the first two stages of alfalfa's life cycle. (And you can add the results to your salad.)

Have Some MORE Fun!

Bonus Activity 1:
Order a "triops" kit. (Inexpensive kits are readily available online.) Also known as "dinosaur shrimp", these ancient creatures look like tiny horseshoe crabs and are great fun to watch. The kit will allow you to observe a full life cycle as triops hatch from eggs, grow to adults, reproduce, and eventually die.

Bonus Activity 2:
Research various life cycles. Compare very short life cycles (like mayflies) with very long life cycles (like bristlecone pines). Focus on how insect life cycles differ from the life cycles of plants, then compare this to the life cycles of various animals.

National Standards

Here are the National Standards reflected in this chapter:

"Plants and animals have life cycles that include being born, developing into adults, reproducing, and eventually dying. The details of this life cycle are different for different organisms. Plants and animals closely resemble their parents."
   — **National Science Education Standards** (C2.A) (C2.B)

"Plants and animals have unique and diverse life cycles. Adult plants and animals can have young. Young animals are very much, but not exactly like, their parents. Plants also are very much, but not exactly, like their parents. Reproduction is essential to the continued existence of every kind of organism."
   — **Next Generation Science Standards** (LS1.B) (LS3.A)

What You Learned

• All plants and animals have life cycles.

• Life cycles often include four major stages.

• Life cycle details are different for different organisms.

• Plants and animals closely resemble their parents.

Preview

Ever been on a cross-country bus trip with a group of high school kids? At first, the bus is clean, everyone is comfortable, and spirits are high. After a few hours, however, the atmosphere starts to deteriorate. Students begin to get fidgety and restless. Candy wrappers and empty soda bottles start piling up. Sweaty bodies and tight quarters quickly compound the problem. Now imagine what it would be like if you were stuck on the bus for days!*

The confined quarters of a bus are like an ecosystem. Links and interactions between living and non-living components create a vibrant dynamic — for better or worse!

Essential Concepts

Earth has millions of different ecosystems. They can be as small as a drop of water, or as large as the earth itself. Scientists often divide ecosystems into groups for study. This can help them more effectively evaluate the interactions taking place within a particular ecosystem.

To better understand the concept of ecosystems, this chapter will focus on one specific type of ecosystem called a biome (pronounced "by' ohm").

A biome is a large ecosystem with certain kinds of plants and animals and a very specific climate. The earth can be divided into six major biomes: forest, grassland, desert, tundra, freshwater, and marine.**

*scenes from the show "Hoarders" pale by comparison
**although "dorm room" certainly deserves consideration

Forests are areas that are dominated by trees. Forests cover about one third of the earth's total land surface. Examples include the rainforests of South America, the northern forests of Canada, and the woods of Wisconsin.

Grasslands are areas where grasses predominate (instead of shrubs or trees). Many grasslands are used to grow crops like wheat or corn. Examples of grasslands include the prairies of America, the savannas of Africa, and the steppes of Russia.

Deserts are areas with very little rainfall. Desert plants and animals must be able to survive with very little water. Examples of major deserts include the Mohave Desert in America, the Sahara Desert in Africa, and (surprisingly) Antarctica.

Tundras are very cold. They have very little precipitation and poor nutrients. Plants are short and tend to group together. Arctic tundras are on lands that circle the North Pole. Alpine tundras are located on mountain tops above the treeline.

Marine biomes are the largest biome, covering over three quarters of Earth's surface. These saltwater environments are filled with many kinds of life.* Examples include oceans, coral reefs, and estuaries (inlets of the sea that mingle with the ends of rivers).

Freshwater biomes can be as small as a pond or as large as Lake Superior. Unlike marine biomes, they contain little salt. Examples include ponds, lakes, streams, rivers, and wetlands. These environments can be found throughout the world.

Each of these biomes is constantly changing due to millions of interactions. In addition, changes in heat, light, or moisture may impact behavior of organisms living in the biome. Other factors, like how many creatures are present, or how much food is available also affect behavior.**

*not including Sponge Bob and Patrick
**For proof, observe the creatures that inhabit any high school prom.

When there are changes to an ecosystem, the plants and animals that live there must change or move away in order to survive. For example, when a lake dries up or becomes polluted, the fish in that lake often die because they can't change and they can't swim away.

All of this has implications not only for biomes, but also for Earth as a whole. As someone once said, "You can't throw anything away, because there *is* no away!"

Protecting ecosystems, both big and small, not only helps the creatures that live there, but also helps conserve vital resources for our future generations.

Have Some Fun!

Make a "Bottle Biome." You'll need a clean 2-liter bottle, some pebbles, potting soil, grass seeds, and water. Cut the top half off the bottle and set it aside. Place a layer of pebbles in the bottom of the bottle, then add a three inch layer of potting soil. Make a shallow trench in the soil and plant the grass seed. Water until you see that the pebbles are covered. Tape the capped top back onto the bottle. Place your mini-biome in a warm, sunny place and wait a few days. This tiny ecosystem models a real biome. If conditions are right, moisture should condense on the top and drip off as "rain" making the grass sprout.

Have Some MORE Fun!

Bonus Activity 1:
Learn the "3 R's" of environmental awareness — reduce, reuse, and recycle. Make a list of ways you can implement this in your life. Remember, that while recyling is great, reusing or repurposing an item is even better. Sites like Pinterest have a variety of very cool projects based on this philosophy.

Bonus Activity 2:
Keep a record of how many aluminum cans you use in one week. Multiply that times the local population times fifty-two to estimate how many cans your community uses in one year. Besides recyling aluminum cans, what are some other ways you could reduce stress on your local ecosystem?

National Standards

Here are the National Standards reflected in this chapter:

"An organism's patterns of behavior are related to the nature of that organism's environment [ecosystem], including the kinds and numbers of other organisms present, the availability of food and resources, and the physical characteristics of the environment."
— **National Science Education Standards** (C1.A)

"There are many different kinds of living things in any area, and they exist in different places on land and in water. A healthy ecosystem is one in which multiple species of different types are each able to meet their needs in a relatively stable web of life."
— **Next Generation Science Standards** (LS1.C) (LS2.A)

What You Learned

• There are many different kinds of ecosystems.

• All living things interact with their ecosystems.

• Scientists call a large, regional ecosystem a "biome".

• When ecosystems change, creatures must adapt or move away in order to survive.

Ecosystem Change

Preview

Describe the "ecosystem" of your home. Start by making a list of the things you see in your house and yard, then add influences like air temperature, lighting, social factors, etc. Now consider how your ecosystem might be different. What changes could you make that might be helpful?" (add a good sound system*, plant trees, etc.) What changes could you make that might be harmful? (turn off all utilities, let trash pile up in your yard, etc.) This illustrates how humans can change their natural and constructed environments for better or worse.

Essential Concepts

All living things cause changes in their environment.** Some of these changes can be helpful; some can be harmful. One of the best ways to gain a clearer understanding of this concept is to look at several examples.

Algae are simple plants that many water creatures rely on for food. But algae can also have a negative impact on an ecosystem. When algae multiply too fast, scientists call it a "bloom." Algae blooms can result in the deaths of thousands of fish and birds, and even some mammals.

Corals usually have a positive impact on marine ecosystems. These tiny creatures live in huge colonies in shallow oceans. Coral reefs are rich with life. They provide an ideal habitat for many creatures — from fish to sea stars to sharks.

*think Mozart, not Megadeth
**especially if they own large construction equipment painted yellow

Kudzu is a perennial vine imported from Southeast Asia. Kudzu thrives in the American south, but has a very negative impact on local ecosystems. These lush vines grow rapidly, covering acres of ground. Once kudzu takes hold, it can completely choke out native vegetation. Most birds and animals must leave to survive.

Trees often have a strong positive impact on an ecosystem. One mature tree produces more oxygen than ten people breathe in a year. Trees also slow storm runoff, serve as windbreaks, and offer cooling shade. A great way to spend a hot summer afternoon is to sit under a shade tree.*

Nutria were imported from South America for the fur farming industry. They look like small beavers with tails like muskrats, and have large, orange teeth.** But nutria multiply rapidly and eat most of the vegetation in an area. Nutria burrows weaken levees and dams, and they destroy native habitat. It's been estimated that even if all the nutria in the South suddenly disappeared, fragile wetlands would take years to recover.

By contrast, beavers can have a positive impact on an ecosystem. They build dams, creating shallow ponds of slow-moving water. These ponds are excellent for wetland growth. The increased vegetation more than makes up for what the beavers eat.

Humans not only depend on the natural ecosystems around them, but also on the ecosystems they construct. Both natural and constructed ecosystems are constantly changing. Positive change often requires good planning and hard work.***

For example, a city park is a natural ecosystem. Tall green trees, beautiful flowers, and grassy lawns make it a nice place to relax. But if a park is not maintained, its ecosystem changes quickly. Trash, weeds, and piles of junk can make a park hazardous.

*Cold ice tea makes this even better.
**Carnivals used to exhibit nutria, claiming they were sewer rats from New York City!
***qualities sometimes as endangered as ecosystems

A house is a type of constructed ecosystem. A well-built house can keep you warm and dry, providing a healthy place to live. But if a house is not cared for, this can change quickly. Moldy walls, leaky roofs, and rotting boards can be very dangerous.

Humans usually have a greater impact on ecosystems than any other creature on Earth. Our actions can be either hurtful or helpful. Importing kudzu and nutria made some ecosystems much worse. But protecting coral reefs is making some ecosystems much better. Remember, small changes to an ecosystem add up quickly. Why not look for ways to improve the ecosystem where you live?

Have Some Fun!

After reading this chapter, you might draw the conclusion that a specific plant or creature is "bad" or "good." But everything on Earth has a role to play in its proper environment. That's what balanced ecosytems are all about.

To emphasize the importance of biodiversity, research the positive characteristics of nutria. What purpose do they serve in the ecosystem of South America? Why are they a serious problem in states like Louisiana, but not in Argentina?

By contrast, research some negative things about beavers. Under what circumstances can this generally beneficial creature become a serious problem? How does urban sprawl and rapid development factor into the situation?

Have Some MORE Fun!

Bonus Activity:
In the last chapter, we talked about the differences between repurposing and recycling, and how the former has less impact on the local ecosystem. For this activity, repurpose at least

one item that might otherwise end up in your local landfill. Etsy, Pinterest, and similar sites are great places to get some inspiration. You'd be surprised at how much money some people make by creatively "repurposing" items!

National Standards

Here are the National Standards reflected in this chapter:

"All organisms cause changes in the environment where they live. Some of these changes are detrimental to the organism or other organisms, whereas others are beneficial."
— **National Science Education Standards** (C1.A)

"Ecosystems are dynamic in nature; their characteristics can vary over time. Disruptions to any physical or biological component of an ecosystem can lead to shifts in all its populations Predatory interactions may reduce the number of organisms or eliminate whole populations of organisms. Mutually beneficial interactions, in contrast, may become so interdependent that each organism requires the other for survival."
— **Next Generation Science Standards** (LS2.A)

What You Learned

• All organisms cause changes in their ecosystems.

• Changes can be harmful or helpful to the organism or to others.

• Humans depend on natural and constructed ecosystems.

• Humans can change their ecosystems for better or worse.

Preview

What did you have for dinner last night? Make a list of the ingredients.* Now divide these items into two groups — "plant-based foods" and "animal-based foods." For example, spaghetti and meatballs could be divided as pasta (plant-based), tomato sauce (plant-based), and meatballs (animal-based).

Now think about the animal-based foods on your list. Where did the nutrition in the meat come from? In other words, the meat obviously came from some sort of animal — but where did the animal get *its* nutrition?

This complex process of interconnectivity is one we seldom think about. In this chapter, we'll look at how the process works, and why its stability is vital to life on Earth.

Essential Concepts

Food webs lie at the heart of every ecosystem. A food web is a complex system composed of all the paths that energy and nutrients can take as they move through an ecosystem. The food webs of different biomes look very different, but they all function in much the same way.

Every food web begins with "autotrophs". Plants are the most common of these, but algae and phytoplankton are autotrophs, too. Autotrophs are vital to the life cycle because they are the only living things that can make their own food!** This means they are not dependent on other organisms for nutrition.

*just basic ingredients, not stuff like Butylated Hydroxytoluene
**apparently there are no teenage autotrophs

Scientists refer to organisms at this level of the food web as ***producers***.

But if producers don't get their nutrition from other organisms, how do they survive? Most plants produce their own food through the process of photosynthesis (although a few rare autotrophs use chemosynthesis). Photosynthesis is a complex activity that combines light energy from the sun, water gathered by the roots, chemicals from the air, and chlorophyll from within the plant's cells.

But fortunately for us, plants don't just feed themselves. Plants are the primary food source for all other creatures on Earth. All animals, including humans, must consume plants directly or indirectly in order to survive. Scientists refer to organisms at this level of the food web as ***consumers***.

Some consumers (herbivores) get their food directly from plants. They do this by eating plants or plant products. For example, parrots and cockatoos eat seeds, fruits, and flower buds. Cattle and deer eat grasses and grains. Hummingbirds drink flower nectar and tree sap. Giraffes eat leaves and twigs. Squirrels eat nuts, and does eat oats.*

Other consumers (carnivores) get their food indirectly from plants. They do this by eating the animals that ate the plants. When a hawk eats a mouse, it gets nutrition indirectly from any grain or seeds the mouse may have eaten. When a wolf eats a rabbit, it gets nutrition indirectly from the vegetation the rabbit has been eating. When you eat a hamburger, you get nutrition indirectly from the grass and hay that the cow fed on.

The third group, ***eecomposers***, are the organisms that function at the last level of the food web. The most common decomposers are bacteria and fungi, but this level also includes creatures like earthworms, termites, and dung beetles.

*and little lambs eat ivy

All decomposers use various types of waste materials or dead organisms for their food. The ability of decomposers to turn organic waste into inorganic material helps return nutrients to the soil and oceans for use by autotrophs.

When the decomposition process is finished, the energy flow through the ecosystem starts over again — from autotrophs to consumers to decomposers. In a healthy ecosystem, this constant flow of energy allows the needs of multiple species to be met through a stable food web.

Have Some Fun!

Watch a video or film that illustrates the close connection between plants and animals. (There are hundreds of titles available online — or check your local library.) An excellent example is *The Private Life of Plants*. Episode 5 of this BBC series specifically focuses on plant/animal dependencies.

Have Some MORE Fun!

Bonus Activity:
Spend some time with an avid gardener. Ask him/her to show you samples of things that he/she has grown. Talk about the wide variety of food plants that can be grown in a home garden, and the special needs these plants have in order to thrive.

National Standards

Here are the National Standards reflected in this chapter:

"Populations of organisms can be categorized by the function they serve in an ecosystem. Plants are producers—they make their own food. All animals, including humans, are consumers, which obtain

food by eating other organisms. Decomposers, primarily bacteria and fungi, use waste materials and dead organisms for food. Energy flows through ecosystems in one direction, from photosynthetic organisms to herbivores to carnivores to decomposers."
— **National Science Education Standards** (C4.B)

"The food of almost any kind of animal can be traced back to plants. Organisms are related in food webs in which some animals eat plants for food and other animals eat the animals that eat plants. Some organisms, such as fungi and bacteria, break down dead organisms and therefore operate as decomposers. Decomposition eventually restores some materials back to the soil. A healthy ecosystem is one in which multiple species of different types are each able to meet their needs in a relatively stable web of life."
— **Next Generation Science Standards** (LS2.A)

What You Learned

• Food webs have three basic levels: autotrophs, consumers, and decomposers.

• *Autotrophs* (like plants) are the only organisms that make their own food.

• *Consumers* (both herbivores and carnivores) need plants to survive.

• *Decomposers* (like bacteria) turn organic wastes into inorganic materials.

• Healthy ecosystems require a relatively stable food web.

Heredity

Preview

Some characteristics are natural. You inherit them from your parents and grandparents. These can include eye color, nearsightedness, and whether or not you have dimples.* Other characteristics are learned. This means they are developed over time through interaction with your environment.

Simple, right? But if someone is an excellent mechanic, chances are that a parent or grandparent may have been an excellent mechanic, too. So is mechanical skill an inherited or a learned characteristic? That's what we'll explore in this chapter.

Essential Concepts

As stated above, all organisms are a combination of various characteristics. Some are natural; some are learned.

Natural characteristics are inherited. They are passed down from parents to their offspring. For example, if you have blue eyes, then one of your ancestors had blue eyes, too.

Learned characteristics are not inherited. We learn them from interaction with our environment. Even if one of your parents was a chess master, you can't simply inherit a knowledge of how to play the game.**

To gain a clearer understanding of this concept, let's look at some specific examples.

*dents in the skin that are considered cute ... although no one knows why
**and you're probably more interested in Minecraft anyway

A parrot can use its beak and claws to manipulate objects. This is an inherited characteristic. But if you've ever been on a vacation to Florida, you may have seen parrots that someone trained to ride tiny bicycles!* This is a learned characteristic, and it can't be inherited.

Dolphins forage for fish and squid along shorelines and coves. Foraging is an inherited characteristic. But scientists have found that some dolphins teach their young to protect their snouts with a sponge while foraging. This is a learned behavior.

Toy poodles are small dogs with dense, curly hair and relatively long legs. These are inherited characteristics. But some poodles have been trained to dance on their hind legs. This characteristic is learned, and it can't be inherited by their pups.

Gorillas are born with flexible hands that can easily manipulate objects. This is an inherited characteristic of gorillas. Researchers taught one gorilla, named Koko, how to use her flexible hands for sign language. But this learned skill can't be inherited.

Closer to home, a person's hair type (curly, wavy, or straight) is an inherited characteristic. But how you wear your hair (long, short, spiked) is a learned characteristic. Teenage hairstyles seldom reflect the hairstyles of their parents!

What about the question we asked in the Preview? Is mechanical skill inherited or learned? The answer is both! A mechanic may have inherited abilities in spatial memory and manual dexterity from a parent or grandparent. But he or she still has to learn and practice specific mechanical skills in order to become truly proficient. Most skills and abilities are a *combination* of inherited and learned characteristics. (This is a point that many textbooks fail to emphasize.)

*a phenomenon similar to dimples

It's also important to note that natural characteristics are not always helpful. For example, you may have inherited a predisposition to diabetes or heart disease. But proper diet and exercise can help fight these problems. A healthy lifestyle is one of the best learned characteristics!

Have Some Fun!

You'll need a small jar, a small flower pot, a spoonful of lentils, potting soil, water, and plastic wrap. Fill the flower pot half full of potting soil. Soak the lentils in the jar overnight.

The next day, drain the lentils and choose three to plant as seeds. Space the seeds on the soil, then press them down until they are covered. Water them gently, then cover the top of the pot with plastic wrap. Place the pot in a warm, sunny location. After the seeds sprout (three or four days), make daily notes about each plant's characteristics. Carefully monitor for individual changes.

This activity lets you compare inherited characteristics (the type of plant, general size, shape, color, etc.) with learned characteristics (how each plant responds to its environment).

Have Some MORE Fun!

Bonus Activity 1:
To expand your understanding of *inherited* characteristics, check out the historic work of Gregor Mendel. Research his experiments with pea plants, then explore how his findings contributed to the modern science of genetics.

Bonus Activity 2:
To expand your understanding of *learned* characteristics, learn to play the ancient game of Mancala. (You can find the rules on the Internet.) Although beautiful wooden game boards are available,

all you really need are some pebbles or seeds and some circles drawn on paper or in the dirt. Be sure to reflect on how skill at this game cannot be inherited.

National Standards

Here are the National Standards reflected in this chapter:

"Many characteristics of an organism are inherited from the parents of the organism, but other characteristics result from an individual's interactions with the environment. Inherited characteristics include the color of flowers and the number of limbs of an animal. Other features, such as the ability to ride a bicycle, are learned through interactions with the environment and cannot be passed on to the next generation."
— **National Science Education Standards** (C1.A)

"Many characteristics of organisms are inherited from their parents. Other characteristics result from individuals' interactions with the environment, which can range from diet to learning. Many characteristics involve both inheritance and environment. Different organisms vary in how they look and function because they have different inherited information."
— **Next Generation Science Standards** (LS3.A) (LS3.B)

What You Learned

• Some characteristics are natural (inherited). Natural characteristics come through an organism's parents.

• Some characteristics are learned (environmental). Learned characteristics come from an organism's interaction with its environment.

• Many skills and abilities are a combination of inherited and learned characteristics.

Behaviors

Preview

Humans and animals behave in certain ways. Some behaviors are influenced by feelings inside us. These are called *internal cues*. Other behaviors are influenced by the things around us. These are called *external cues*.

Behaviors like geese flying south in the winter, or a cow grazing on grass are based on such cues. So are behaviors like putting on your coat when you're cold, or getting a drink of water when you're thirsty. In this chapter, we'll explore various human and animal behaviors and their scientific causes.

Essential Concepts

Humans and animals engage in many kinds of activities, and most of these activities can be observed. Scientists refer to observable actions by humans and animals *behaviors*. Sometimes behaviors are acceptable, and sometimes they're not.* But all behaviors have one thing in common: They are a reaction to some kind of an influence.

Behaviors can be influenced by feelings inside us. Scientists call these *internal cues*. Hunger is one type of internal cue. When an animal is hungry, it looks for something to eat.** Thirst is another internal cue. When you are thirsty, you look for something cold to drink. Fatigue is also an internal cue. When you need to rest, you look for somewhere quiet to sleep.

*Just ask Miley Cyrus.
**a continuous behavior for teenage males

Behaviors are also influenced by the things around us. Scientists call these *external cues*. Temperature can be an external cue. When you get too hot, you look for a quick way to cool off. Availability of food can be another external cue. When food becomes scarce, animals tend to move elsewhere. Sunlight can also be an external cue. When the days become shorter, geese fly south for the winter.*

Behavioral cues can also be either voluntary or involuntary. Lighting a fire is a voluntary behavior. But pulling your hand back from a sudden burst of flames is an involuntary behavior based on an external cue.

All living creatures have various senses that help them detect different types of external cues. Here are some examples:

• A hawk's eyes help it detect movement. A running mouse is an external cue that may lead the hawk to food.

• A rabbit's ears help it detect danger. The howl of a wolf is an urgent external cue for the rabbit to disappear.

• A rescue dog's nose can help it detect people in trouble. The scent of an injured person serves as a strong external cue.

• To a raccoon, touch is a vital sense. External cues from touch help a raccoon identify objects and solve tricky problems.

• A monitor lizard's tongue allows it to taste the air. This external cue can help the lizard detect movement and prey.

There are also a number of *internal* cues that scientists don't fully understand — like fish migration patterns, or the "biological clock" that many creatures seem to have.**

*where they try to beat retired Minnesotans to the best RV spots

**or the urge of adult humans to do the "chicken dance"

For example, why do internal cues cause a thirty-pound Coho salmon to batter it's way miles upstream to spawn? And what kind of internal cues tell chipmunks, turtles, and bears when to emerge from hibernation?

Internal and external cues affect the behavior of almost every living thing. See if you can detect examples in the people and animals around you.

Have Some Fun!

You'll need three paper cups, and one tablespoon each of salt, sugar, and flour. Put a tablespoon of salt in Cup A, a tablespoon of sugar in Cup B, and a tablespoon of flour in Cup C. Close your eyes and have a friend place one of the cups under your nose. Smell the material and try to guess what it is. Have your friend write down your guess. Repeat with the other two cups.

Now repeat the entire procedure, only this time use your fingers instead of your nose. Have your friend write this set of guesses in a second column.

Finally, open your eyes and look in each cup. Have your friend write down your final guesses, then compare the columns of answers. Notice that as you use more senses (smell, touch, sight), your ability to identify the materials increases. This helps show the relationship between senses and external cues.

Have Some MORE Fun!

Bonus Activity:
Talk with an animal behavior expert (naturalist, forest ranger, zookeeper, etc.) about various animal behaviors that he/she has seen or studied. Discuss how those behaviors can be helpful or harmful to the animal. See if you can identify the internal and external cues involved.

National Standards

Here are the National Standards reflected in this chapter:

"The behavior of individual organisms is influenced by internal cues (such as hunger) and by external cues (such as a change in the environments). Humans and other organisms have senses that help them detect internal and external cues."
— **National Science Education Standards** (C1.D)

"Plants and animals have both internal and external structures that serve various functions in growth, survival, behavior, and reproduction. Sense receptors respond to different inputs (electromagnetic, mechanical, chemical), transmitting them as signals that travel along nerve cells to the brain. The signals are then processed in the brain, resulting in behaviors."
— **Next Generation Science Standards** (LS1.A) (LS1.D)

What You Learned

• Humans and animals behave in observable ways.

• Behaviors can be influenced by internal cues.

• Behaviors can be influenced by external cues.

• A creature's sense receptors help it detect such cues.

Earth & Space Science

"The scientific theory I like best is that the rings of Saturn are composed entirely of lost airline luggage."

- Mark Russell

The Sun

Preview

Imagine you're walking barefoot across your front lawn on a sunny summer day. You wave at a friend across the street, then walk over to meet her. You step onto the street and ... *Youch!*

Most of us have experienced this "asphalt hot foot" at one time or another. But since both the street and the grass are in direct sunlight, why would the street be hotter than the grass? That's just one of the phenomenon we'll explore in this chapter.

Essential Concepts

The sun is the star in the center of our solar system. It's a huge ball of hot gases and nuclear reactions.* According to scientists, the sun's interior core can reach temperatures of over twenty-five million degrees. Although the sun's surface is much cooler than that, it's still so hot that metals like iron exist only as liquids.

But even though the sun is extremely hot, it doesn't warm the earth like a fire warms us.** The sun is much too far away. Between the earth and the sun, there are millions and millions of miles of cold, airless space.

But if the sun's heat doesn't warm the earth directly, then why isn't our entire world completely frozen? It's because the sun constantly releases another form of energy — sunlight! And fortunately for us, sunlight can be converted into heat.

not to be confused with radio talk show hosts
**see the comments on page 7*

When sunlight strikes an object, it can be reflected, refracted, or absorbed.* When sunlight is absorbed, it produces heat. Usually the more sunlight that an object absorbs, the hotter it gets.

Absorption of light can be affected by color. Objects that have dark, dull colors (like flat black) usually absorb more sunlight. This causes them to get hotter. Objects that have light, shiny colors (like glossy white) absorb much less sunlight. This tends to keep them cooler.

But there are other factors at play, too. When sunlight hits an object directly, the object usually absorbs more light, causing it to get hotter. When sunlight hits an object at an angle, the object absorbs much less light, keeping the object cooler.

That plays a significant role in the seasons.** In summer, the sun passes high overhead. Light from the sun hits that portion of the earth directly. The combination of direct sunlight and longer days results in warmer weather.

In the winter, however, the sun is low on the horizon. Light from the sun hits that part of the earth at an angle. The combination of shorter days and less direct sunlight results in colder weather.

Absorbed sunlight is important in many other ways. Plants on Earth absorb sunlight to help them make food through a process called photosynthesis. Much of life on Earth depends on the food and oxygen produced through this process.

Absorbed sunlight also helps maintain the earth's temperature. Without sunlight being absorbed and converted to heat, life as we know it would cease to exist. The absorption of sunlight even impacts ocean currents and water cycles, which in turn greatly affect Earth's weather.

*See the chapter on "Light."
**We'll talk more about that in the "Weather & Seasons" chapter.

Scientists and inventors have designed many new technologies that are based on absorbed sunlight. Photovoltaic panels can convert sunlight directly into electricity. Commercial or homemade solar collectors can be used to heat water. Solar architects can design a house to take maximum advantage of solar heating, power generation, and more. (Orientation alone can account for huge differences in potential solar gain.)

As you can see, light energy from the sun provides support directly or indirectly for virtually every form of life on Earth.

Have Some Fun!

You'll need two clear glass jars with lids, flat black paint, aluminum foil, and water. Cover Jar #1 with aluminum foil. Paint Jar #2 flat black and allow it to dry overnight.

The next day, fill both jars with water and attach the lids. Place both jars in direct sunlight (a windowsill works great), and let them sit for several hours. Make sure the jars remain in direct sunlight.

Now remove the lids and touch a finger to the water in each jar to compare temperatures. Since dull, dark colors absorb heat much better than light, shiny colors, the water in Jar #2 should be much hotter. This simple demonstration clearly shows how sunlight can be converted to heat.

Have Some MORE Fun!

Bonus Activity:
Recently there have been amazing advances in solar technology. For example, if you live in a suitable location, new companies like SolarCity will convert your home to solar power with no upfront costs. In many markets, this is cheaper than traditional power!

Solar lighting has become commonplace, and some of the newer electric cars even have photovoltaic roofs that recharge their batteries for free.

Although you seldom hear much about solar energy on mainstream media (except for stories about huge commercial projects), a little research can help you discover a wealth of information about ways solar technology is changing energy production, home construction, transportation, and much more.

National Standards

Here are the National Standards reflected in this chapter:

"The sun provides the light and heat necessary to maintain the temperature of the earth. The sun is the major source of energy for phenomena on the earth's surface, such as the growth of plants, winds, ocean currents, and the water cycle."
— **National Science Education Standards** (D2.B)

"The sun is a star that appears larger and brighter than other stars because it is closer. Sunlight warms Earth's surface. Sunlight transfers energy from place to place."
— **Next Generation Science Standards** (PS3.B) (ESS1.A)

What You Learned

• The sun is a huge ball of hot gases and nuclear reactions.

• Most energy from the sun reaches the earth as sunlight.

• When sunlight is absorbed, it can produce heat.

• Different things affect how much sunlight objects absorb.

• Absorbed sunlight impacts Earth's temperature and weather.

The Moon

Preview

According to NASA,* most people seriously misunderstand the phases of the moon. So for this chapter, we'll use the hands-on activity on page 85 as our introduction. Once you've finished that, you'll have a much better foundation for understanding the rest of the chapter, and why the shape of the moon seems to change from night to night.

(Here's a hint: It's not due to the Earth's shadow like many people think. That would be a lunar eclipse.)

Essential Concepts

The moon is Earth's only natural satellite. When the moon is full, it is the brightest object in the night sky.

The moon's surface is covered with rocks and dust. It is very cold and dry, and has no atmosphere to support life. Thousands of craters dot the moon's surface, showing the impact of meteorites. Most of these struck long ago, although hundreds of detectable impacts still occur each year. In fact, an exceptionally large impact was recorded in September of 2013.

The moon is about one fourth the diameter of the earth, making it by far the largest satellite in the Solar System relative to the size of its planet. And although the moon is very tiny when compared to the sun (much smaller than a BB next to a basketball), the moon and sun appear to be about the same size when viewed from Earth. This is because the sun is much farther away.

*the space experts, not the National Auto Sport Association

As the earth rotates, the moon seems to move slowly across the night sky — rising in the east and setting in the west. But although the moon follows a specific path as it orbits the earth, this path is different than that of the sun.

During part of its cycle, the moon is opposite the sun. This means it rises around the same time the sun is setting. But at other times, the moon's path nearly matches the sun's path. If conditions are right, you can see the moon during the day.

The moon's observable shape changes slightly from night to night. Although half the moon is always lit by the sun*, we see that half at different angles as the moon rotates around the earth, giving the illusion of different shapes. Scientists call these different appearances "phases."

There are eight major phases beginning with a *new* moon. No direct light is visible on the portion of the moon we see. The cycle continues with a *waxing crescent* moon, which shows a curved slice of light along the right side of the moon. Next comes the *first quarter* moon, sometimes called a half moon. The entire right half of the moon is illuminated. Then comes the *waxing gibbous* moon** where light appears to cover three-quarters of the right side of the moon. Halfway through the cycle a *full* moon occurs when the moon is on the opposite side of the earth from the sun, and the entire surface facing us is lit up.

The second half of the cycle continues with a *waning gibbous* moon. This resembles the waxing gibbous, except light is on the left side. Then comes the *third quarter* moon — another half moon, but with the light appearing on the moon's left half. The cycle nears its end with a *waning crescent* moon. This is like the waxing crescent but with light on the left. And finally, we're back to a new moon again.

*Sorry, classic rock fans ... there is no "dark side of the moon".
**which maketh the gibbons speak gibberish

Remember, the sun is always shining on one half of the moon (except during an eclipse). Moon phases are just a way to describe what's happening to the part we see. Phases of the moon always occur in this pattern, and the pattern begins anew about every thirty days. So observe the moon on the next clear night, then see if you can figure out what the next phase will be.

Have Some Fun!

You'll need a styrofoam ball (to represent the moon), a bright flashlight (to represent the sun), a pencil, and a darkened room. To prepare, stick the pencil into the center of the styrofoam ball to make a handle, and place the flashlight on a shelf at one side of the room (at or above eye level). Make sure the flashlight is pointed toward the center of the room.

Now turn on the flashlight, and stand in the center of the room. (You represent the Earth.) With your back to the light, hold the ball in front of you and slightly above your head. The side of the ball toward you will be covered with light, simulating a *full* moon. Now turn around and face the flashlight. The side of the ball toward you is now in full shadow. This simulates a *new* moon. As you read through this chapter, use this model to simulate all eight phases of the moon.

Have Some MORE Fun!

Bonus Activity 1:
Keep a "moon journal" beginning with the next new moon. On a sheet of paper, draw 30 blank circles. Shade one circle each night to represent what you see, and write the date below it. (If the moon can't be seen due to inclement weather, put an "X" on that circle.) Compare your observations throughout the month. Sites like **http://stardate.org/nightsky/moon** offer wonderful tools to support this activity.

Bonus Activity 2:
Research the difference between a "new moon" and a "full moon."
Verify that you know what these opposite phases look like, then
find out when each one normally rises and sets. For extra fun,
research what the term "blue moon" means.

National Standards

Here are the National Standards reflected in this chapter:

*"The moon moves across the sky on a daily basis much like the sun.
The observable shape of the moon change from day to day in a cycle
that lasts about a month."*
          — **National Science Education Standards** (D3.C)

*"Patterns of the motion of the sun, moon, and stars in the sky can be
observed, described, and predicted. The orbits of Earth around the
sun and of the moon around Earth ... cause observable patterns. These
include day and night ... and different positions of the sun, moon,
and stars at different times of the day, month, and year."*
          — **Next Generation Science Standards** (ESS1.A) (ESS2.A)

What You Learned

• The moon is Earth's only natural satellite.

• The moon is about one fourth the diameter of the earth.

• The moon's observable shape changes slightly each night.

• This cycle of change takes about 30 days.

Earth Resources

Preview

Just like we did in the last chapter, we'll use a hands-on activity to introduce this lesson. Once you finish working the **Cookie Mine** on page 89, you can better visualize some of the pressing issues in the management of natural resources.

Essential Concepts

Earth is blessed with an abundance of natural resources. Many of these resources help provide essential materials that humans need to survive. Let's look at some examples.

Rocks are a natural resource. Rocks can be hard or soft, light or heavy, rough or smooth. Some rocks are formed by extreme heat and pressure (metamorphic); some come from sediments (sedimentary); some are made of volcanic material (igneous).

Soil is a natural resource. Soil is made from organic substances like dead plants, and inorganic substances like rocks or sand. Soils have different colors and textures. Soils also vary in their nutrient values or their ability to absorb water.

Water is a natural resource. More than seventy percent of Earth's surface is covered with different types of water. Fresh water areas include lakes, rivers, and wetlands. Salt water areas include oceans, coral reefs, and estuaries.

Air is a natural resource. The air we breathe is composed primarily of oxygen, nitrogen, and carbon dioxide gases.*

plus a variety of mystery ingredients if you live in Los Angeles

A moving layer of air surrounds the earth. This air helps control temperature and moisture, and makes weather patterns.

The natural materials that we use as resources have different physical and chemical properties. These properties can be helpful in many different ways.

For example, the properties of *rocks* make them useful as building materials. Limestone, granite, marble, and similar rocks are common in construction. Other rocks, called ores, contain minerals like copper or iron that are used to make metals. There are even some types of rocks, like anthracite coal, that can be burned as fuel.*

The properties of *soil* make it another important resource. But soil can be damaged by too much water or wind. Most of today's farmers use methods designed to protect the soil. Good soil means healthier plants, and healthier plants make better food. This is just one way soil helps people and animals survive.

Of course, *water* is an important natural resource, too.** All living things need water to survive. Not only do you drink water, but over half of your body is made of water! Water is used to irrigate crops and process food. Water is also used in making everything from cakes to clothing to cars.

Our most vital natural resource is *air*. Virtually all life on Earth needs air to survive. But air can also be used in many other ways. Factories use air to run tools. Warehouses use cold air to keep foods frozen. Air supports airplanes when they fly.

Rocks, soil, water, and air are just a few of Earth's natural resources. Others include wood, natural fibers, and materials like clay. Humans take these resources and process them in various ways to make the products we use every day.

Just don't build a fire pit out of anthracite!
**ask any fisherman*

Natural materials are a wonderful resource, but they must be used wisely. Look for ways you can implement the "3 R's" of environmental awareness — reduce, reuse, and recycle — and help conserve Earth's natural riches.

Have Some Fun!

Welcome **Cookie Miner**! You'll need two raisin cookies, two paper plates, and a toothpick. (The cookies represent mining environments; the raisins represent resources.) Place a raisin cookie on each plate. Using only a toothpick, mine Cookie #1 to remove whole raisins while damaging the cookie as little as possible. Next mine Cookie #2. This time remove as many whole raisins as you can, regardless of damage to the cookie.

Once you're finished, compare the "production totals" (count only whole raisins) versus the "environmental damage" for each cookie. This activity demonstrates how different goals can significantly impact an ecosystem.

Have Some MORE Fun!

Bonus Activity 1:
Watch a documentary about the historic Oklahoma "dust bowl" era or another major drought. How does this relate to current concerns scientists have about water availability in our western states? (Exploring information on the Colorado River Delta would be a good place to start.)

Bonus Activity 2:
Research natural resources that are essential for plant growth (soil, water, air). How does the quality and quantity of these materials affect plants? Pay special attention to how changing conditions may impact America's major food crops in the future.

National Standards

Here are the National Standards reflected in this chapter:

"Earth materials are solid rocks and soils, water, and the gases of the atmosphere. These varied materials have different physical and chemical properties, which make them useful in different ways, for example as building materials, as sources of fuel, or for growing the plants we use as food. Earth materials provide many of the resources humans use."
— **National Science Education Standards** (D1.A)

"Humans depend on Earth's land, ocean, atmosphere, and biosphere for many different resources. Minerals, fresh water, and biosphere resources are limited, and many are not renewable or replaceable over human lifetimes. These resources are distributed unevenly around the planet as a result of past geologic processes."
— **Next Generation Science Standards** (ESS3.A)

What You Learned

- Earth's natural resources include rocks, soils, water, and atmospheric gases.

- Earth's natural resources have different physical and chemical properties.

- Different properties make these natural resources useful in many different ways.

- Earth's natural resources are limited, and many of them are not renewable within our lifetimes.

Preview

In the last chapter, we explored Earth's natural resources, including rocks, soil, water, and air. In the next two chapters, we'll take a closer look at two of these important resources — water and soil.

Essential Concepts

First, the basics. Water covers the majority of Earth's surface. It circulates through the crust, oceans, and atmosphere. It is found in oceans, lakes, rivers, wetlands, and the atmosphere. It can also be found in glaciers and underground.

But even though water is abundant, the amount of water on Earth is finite. In other words, we can't make or produce water. What we have is what we have.

Nearly all of Earth's accessible water is in its oceans.* Most of Earth's *fresh* water is trapped in glaciers or underground. Only a tiny fraction is found in streams, lakes, ponds, wetlands, and the atmosphere. We'll talk more about that in a moment.

Water has many unique properties that make it critical to Earth's systems. Liquid water has the ability to absorb, store, and release large amounts of energy. It also can dissolve and transport many types of materials. It can even lower the melting point of rocks.

Water's non-liquid states are also important. As we discussed in Chapter 1, water can change states with relative ease.** At room

*which are saltier than movie theatre popcorn
**from solid to liquid to gas ... not from Kansas to Nebraska

temperature, water is a liquid. But when water gets cold enough, it expands and turns into a solid (ice, sleet, hail, etc.). When heated, it can turn into a gas (steam). Then as steam cools, it turns back into liquid water. This ability to easily change states makes water useful in a variety of ways.

Water moves around the planet in a process that scientists call the "water cycle."* It evaporates, rises and cools, condenses, and falls back to the surface. A common misconception is that this process only involves open water (lakes, rivers, and the ocean). But water can also evaporate from plants, animals, and even the soil itself. In addition, the global water cycle also includes ice in all its forms (glaciers, sea ice, icebergs, permafrost, etc.).

The water cycle is a very complex process, and major shifts can occur over time. Unfortunately, a combination of climate change and overconsumption has created critical water shortages in many parts of the world. Thousands die each year from major droughts, and in America, many western states are beginning to face serious water shortages.

In addition, experts estimate water consumption will continue to double every twenty years. That means that in less than a decade, over 30% of Earth's people may no longer have access to adequate drinking water! Since diseases from unsafe water already kill more people every year than all forms of violence (including war), this growing crisis is a recipe for disaster.**

Because of its increasing scarcity, some people are starting to refer to fresh water as "the new oil." But unlike oil, there are no viable alternatives to potable water.

Also, many so-called "solutions" can create even more problems. For example, bottled water sales have skyrocketed in recent years. Yet its production and transportation uses the equivalent of 50

*not to be confused with a personal watercraft
**and the storyline for some very scary novels

million barrels of oil a year, and over a million tons of plastic end up in landfills. And few people realize that municipal tap water is actually more regulated (EPA) than bottled water (FDA).

As serious water issues increasing gain the attention of governments, industry, and entrepreneurs, it's important that everyone involved clearly understand these key concepts about water and its related issues. Only in this way can we effectively address the challenges our world will face in the future.

Have Some Fun!

You'll need two clear plastic cups, a tablespoon, some tape, and water. Put two tablespoons of water into Cup A. Place Cup B upside down on Cup A, then tape them together. Place this simple "condensation chamber" in a warm, sunny window for three hours.

Now observe what has happened to the surface of Cup B. This activity demonstrates the role that sunlight plays in the process of condensation.

Have Some MORE Fun!

Bonus Activity 1:
Research some of the problems and potential solutions to the ongoing water crisis in America's western states. Some areas to focus on include aging infrastructure (pipes), water conservation, and agricultural management plans. Find out about the group "greywater guerrillas" and explore their goals.

Bonus Activity 2:
Research the issues surrounding the use of bottled water. What are the arguments for and against its use? How might your findings affect future actions of you or your friends?

National Standards

Here are the National Standards reflected in this chapter:

"Water, which covers the majority of the earth's surface, circulates through the crust, oceans, and atmosphere in what is known as the 'water cycle'. Water evaporates form the earth's surface, rises and cools as it moves to higher elevations, condenses are rain or snow, and falls to the surface where it collects in lakes, oceans, soil, and in rocks underground."
— **National Science Education Standards** (D1.F)

"Water is found in the ocean, rivers, lakes, and ponds. Water exists as solid ice and in liquid form. Nearly all of Earth's available water is in the ocean. Most fresh water is in glaciers or underground; only a tiny fraction is in streams, lakes, wetlands, and the atmosphere. Water continually cycles among land, ocean, and atmosphere via transpiration, evaporation, condensation and crystallization, and precipitation, as well as downhill flows on land. "
— **Next Generation Science Standards** (ESS2.C)

What You Learned

• Water covers the majority of Earth's surface.

• Although abundant, the total amount of water is finite.

• The properties of water make it critical to Earth's systems.

• Water constantly circulates in a process called the "water cycle".

• Only a tiny fraction of Earth's fresh water is readily available.

Preview

Soil is one of our most misunderstood natural resources. After all, it's just dirt, right? But all dirt is not created equal.*

Close your eyes and think about a patch of soil you have seen. Picture it clearly in your mind. Now write a short description of this soil. What color was it? What did it feel like? Was it wet or dry? Focus on descriptive words like rough, smooth, red, black, damp, soggy, and so on. Now repeat this exercise, thinking about a completely different type of soil.

It's important to note that soils not only have different colors and textures, they also differ in other important ways. We'll take a closer look at the properties of soil in this chapter.

Essential Concepts

Soil is primarily a mixture of organic and inorganic materials.** Organic materials are a significant component. Pieces of decayed plant and animal matter add important nutrients to soil.

Soil also contains inorganic materials. Variations in the amount of sand, silt, or clay can greatly affect how soil feels. The specific combination of organic and inorganic materials (plus water and air) is what gives soil properties like color and texture.

Soil color is easy to see. Scientists have identified over 170 different soil colors, the most common shades being black,

* Try scraping red Texas clay off your hiking boots!
** possibly including last night's meatloaf

brown, red, gray, and white. A good gardener can tell a lot about soil just by looking at its color. In general, the darker the soil, the more nutrients it contains. Many types of food plants thrive in darker soils.

Soil texture depends on how much sand, silt, or clay is present. Different combinations mean different textures.

Sand particles are the largest. A large piece of sand is about the size of a grain of salt. Sandy soils feel gritty to the touch. Silt particles are smaller than sand, but larger than clay. When wet, silt has a smooth feel. Clay particles are the smallest. Their dry texture is similar to flour. When wet, clay feels sticky.

Particle size can also affect a soil's capacity to hold water and nutrients. Too much of one type can cause problems. Sandy soils drain quickly, but they don't hold nutrients very well. Clay soils are great at holding nutrients well, but they drain poorly.

Composition of soil varies from place to place. It also changes as materials are added or removed. Different soil compositions support different types of plants. They also affect how well those plants will grow. Here are some examples:

• Many types of berries grow best in sandy soils. This type of soil contains lots of air and also provides good drainage.

• Maple trees do well in soils with a high clay content. This type of soil is closely packed and has lots of nutrients.

• Tomatoes grow best in rich soil called "loam." This type of soil is usually loose, dark, and full of organic matter.

• Cranberries grow best in boggy soil. Bogs are wetlands with very soggy soil that is unsuitable for most other plants.*

*If you're harvesting cranberries, don't get "bogged down" in your work.

Although soil is formed slowly, it can be destroyed rapidly. Too much water or wind can quickly cause major damage. That's why responsible soil management practices are very important.

Most of today's farmers use methods designed to protect the soil. Better soil means healthier plants and more food. Even though it's just "dirt," this natural resource must be used wisely.

Have Some Fun!

You'll need two paper towels (one high quality, one low), and a cup of water. Look closely at the paper towels. How are they similar? How are they different? Predict which towel will absorb water the best. Now test your prediction by dipping small strips of towel into the water and recording the results. What characteristics did the more absorbent towel have compared to the less absorbent towel?

This activity models how differences in composition can affect a material's capacity to retain water. The composition of some soils causes them to hold water better than others.

Have Some MORE Fun!

Bonus Activity 1:
The primary shades of soil are black, brown, red, gray, and white. Research each of these soil colors, and discover what factors might cause a specific color (the presence of certain minerals, high organic content, etc.).

Bonus Activity 2:
Make "dirt desserts." Partially fill clear plastic cups with layers of pudding. (Chocolate and butterscotch are good "dirt" choices.) Top this with a thick layer of crushed chocolate cookies. For even more fun, bury a Gummy Worm in the center of each desert. Be sure to share them with unsuspecting friends.

National Standards

Here are the National Standards reflected in this chapter:

"Earth materials ... have different physical and chemical properties which make them useful in different ways. Soils have properties of color and texture, capacity to retain water, and the ability to support the growth of many kinds of plants."
— **National Science Education Standards** (D1.B)

"The geosphere includes solid and molten rock, soil, and sediments. The sustainability of human societies and the biodiversity that supports them requires responsible management of major natural resources such as the geosphere."
— **Next Generation Science Standards** (ESS2.A) (ESS3.C)

What You Learned

• Soil contains both organic and inorganic materials.

• Soils have different colors and textures.

• Soils differ in their capacity to retain water.

• Different soils support different kinds of plants.

• Responsible soil management practices are very important.

Preview

Think about a time that you walked through the mud. You probably left footprints behind. What did your footprints look like? The shape of your foot or shoe, of course!

A soft surface like mud easily takes an imprint of an object that's pressed into it.* Changes in weather, wind, and water usually make such imprints disappear quickly.

But sometimes rare conditions occur that cause such molds to be preserved. These become the *trace fossils* we find in certain kinds of stone today.

In this chapter, we'll discover three different kinds of fossils and learn how they were formed. We'll also learn how fossils offer clues about ancient environments.

Essential Concepts

Fossils are remains or traces of living things from long ago that have been preserved in the earth's crust. There are fossils of plants, animals, birds, fish, and coral. There are even fossils of things that are difficult to classify.** Fossils offer interesting clues about Earth's ancient past.

One type of fossil is the actual *remains* of an ancient creature. Common fossil remains include teeth, bones, and shells. These hard body parts were often all that was left to become a fossil after the softer body parts rotted away.

*like the hiking boot I lost in the last chapter
**prehistoric twinkies?

Another type of fossil is a stone *replica*. These look very similar to actual remains, only they are made of stone. (Sometimes only a scientist can tell the difference.) This type of fossil was formed when a plant or animal part was slowly replaced with the minerals in the water around it.

A third type of fossil is the evidence that a living thing once existed. These *trace fossils* include nests, dung, tracks, and imprints. Dinosaur tracks in fossilized mud, broken bits of fossilized egg, and similar evidence are all trace fossils.

Most fossils were formed when plants or animals were covered with a thick layer of sediment, like soft mud or clay. The sediment enclosed the remains in a place with little or no air. Without air, the remains could not decompose. A few rare fossils were formed by extremely cold or extremely dry conditions. This can also help stop remains from decomposing.

Fossils come in many sizes. Some, like dinosaur bones, can be very large. Large fossils are often dug up and displayed. But the most common fossils are very small. Many can only be seen through a magnifying glass or a microscope. Scientists call these *microfossils*.

When scientists study fossils, they also discover things about the environment that existed in that place and time. For instance, dinosaur dung (also called coprolite*) helps scientists understand what ancient creatures ate and how they lived.

Fossils also help scientists explore how Earth has changed. Over long periods of time, even huge oceans and mighty mountains move and change. Fossil colonies of ocean creatures are some-times found on mountains, and the teeth of ancient sharks** often show up deep in the desert!

That "polished coprolite" necklace she's wearing is really dinosaur dung!
**also made into unusual necklaces*

But it's important to note that very few ancient plants and animals became fossils when they died. Like today, most living things simply rotted away. Only in rare cases did something happen to preserve part of a plant or animal, or the traces of life that it left behind.

And though countless living things existed in ancient times, relatively little evidence remains. That's why carefully collecting and studying fossils is a very important part of science. Of course, it can be a fun hobby, too!

Have Some Fun!

You'll need a double boiler, a hotplate, paraffin chips, clay, a sea shell, a green leaf, and a chicken bone. (Instructions for making a simple double boiler can be found on the Internet.) Melt the parafin chips in the double boiler. Mold the clay into a pancake shape, then press the shell into the clay to make a mold.

Now carefully pour hot wax into the mold. Wait for the wax to dry, then remove the "fossil" you have made. Smooth the clay, then repeat the process using the leaf, and then the bone.

Once you are through, think about what each part of this activity modeled. The shell, leaf, and bone represent fossilized remains. The impressions in the clay represent trace fossils. And the molded wax represents how replica fossils are formed.

Have Some MORE Fun!

Bonus Activity 1:
Look for fossils near where you live. Any place sedimentary rock is exposed (streambeds, coastlines, cliffs, road cuts, quarries, etc.) is a good place to search. Once you've found some sedimentary rock, use a magnifying glass to look for microfossils. Limestone is common and a great rock for simple fossils like crinoids.

Bonus Activity 2:
Check your local university to see if there is a geologist or paleontologist on staff. Ask him/her to show you samples of various types of fossils. Some universities even have permanent displays open to the public. Encourage him/her to share observations about field work, and find out if there are any fossil-related sites nearby.

National Standards

Here are the National Standards reflected in this chapter:

"Fossils provide evidence about the plants and animals that lived long ago and the nature of the environment at that time."
— **National Science Education Standards** (D1.C)

"The presence and location of certain fossil types indicates the order in which rock layers were formed. The geologic time scale interpreted from rock strata provides a way to organize Earth's history. Analyses of rock strata and the fossil record provide only relative dates, not an absolute scale."
— **Next Generation Science Standards** (ESS1.C)

What You Learned

• Fossils provide evidence about ancient living things and the environment where they lived.

• A fossil can be the actual remains of an ancient living thing.

• A fossil can be a mineralized replica of such remains.

• Trace fossils include nests, dung, and various imprints.

• Fossils are clues that help scientists understand Earth's history.

Earth Changes

Preview

Look at pictures of yourself as a toddler. Compare these to pictures from your first year in school, pictures from the fifth grade, pictures from high school,* and various pictures of you as an adult. It's easy to see some significant physical changes. Some of these changes are huge (changing from a toddler to a fifth grader); others may be barely noticeable (differences between your pictures as an adult).

Just like people, the earth is constantly changing. Some changes are enormous; others are barely noticable. In this chapter, we'll explore such changes and why they occur.

Essential Concepts

All around us, the Earth is changing every day. Some changes happen so slowly we barely notice. Others happen rapidly and are quite dramatic!**

Weathering is an example of a very slow change. Rocks and minerals slowly decompose once they are exposed to the earth's atmosphere. Even though this happens too slowly for us to see, weathering can cause damage to Earth's surface over time. Yet weathering has helpful aspects, too. Materials freed when rocks erode combine with organic materials to create valuable soil.

Erosion is usually a slow change. Erosion occurs as the earth's surface is slowly worn away by water, wind, glaciers, and similar

*You really didn't dress like that, did you?

**hurricanes, volcanoes, and cast changes on Saturday Night Live

forces. But unlike weathering, erosion involves movement. Rocks, soil, and other particles are often carried downslope or downstream for quite some distance.

Sometimes, erosion can happen very rapidly. A major flood can erode soil quickly, often with devastating results. But improved land practices, like building terraces and planting trees, have helped limit many types of erosion.

Landslides are another form of rapid change. A landslide can happen when a slope is weakened and becomes unstable. In 2008, China was hit with several landslides. Some of these blocked rivers, creating dangerous "quake lakes."

Natural causes for landslides include snowmelt, loss of vegetation, heavy rains, earthquakes, and the action of rivers or ocean waves. Occasionally human activities are involved. Heavy construction near any kind of slope must always be planned carefully to avoid causing a landslide.*

Of course, *earthquakes* cause rapid changes, too. Earthquakes occur when the earth's crust suddenly slips or shifts. Although small earthquakes happen all the time, they rarely shake the ground enough to notice. But large earthquakes can cause the surface to crumble or fracture, resulting in enormous damage.

In 1906, a huge earthquake (and subsequent fire) leveled most of San Fransisco. If you visit Point Reyes National Seashore north of town, you can see where the ground shifted several feet.

In 1964, a huge earthquake in Alaska caused streets to buckle, buildings to move, and bridges to collapse. And in 1994, a large earthquake hit the Los Angeles area, injuring thousands and causing over $20 billion in damages.

Land surfing is not a recommended sport.

Volcanoes can also change Earth's surface. Under certain conditions, hot gases trapped in molten rock explode violently. In 1980, Mount St. Helens erupted. The entire top of the mountain blew off, leaving a crater almost two miles wide!

But even though volcanoes can be dangerous, their eruptions add helpful nutrients to the soil over time as volcanic rocks weather away. Volcanoes can also add new land to the earth's surface. Lava pushed out of volcanoes can build mountains, or even create new islands.

Knowing how Earth's surface changes helps scientists better understand the past and what changes to expect in the future.

Have Some Fun!

You'll need a disposable cake pan, a paper cup, sand, water, and a plastic spoon. Pour two cups of sand into one end of the pan. This will represent your "shore." Add one inch of water to the end of the pan opposite the sand. (Be careful not to disturb the sand.) This will represent your "ocean."

Now use the plastic spoon to gently push waves against the shore. Repeat this several times, observing what happens to the shoreline. This activity models waves eroding a sandy shore. Erosion can happen along beaches, lakeshores, riverbanks, or even in the middle of a field after a heavy rain.

Have Some MORE Fun!

Bonus Activity 1:
All volcanoes are not created equal! To demonstrate, label two bottles of soda pop "A" and "B". Open Bottle A and set it aside for a few days until it goes flat. Replace the top, then take both bottles outdoors. Shake each one, then open the tops. Bottle B

will "explode" vigorously. Bottle A will do little or nothing. Even though the liquid in each bottle is similar, the liquid in Bottle A did not have any gas inside to provide energy for an explosion. This is one reason volcanoes in the Pacific Northwest can be quite violent, while volcanoes in Hawaii are relatively tame.

National Standards

Here are the National Standards reflected in this chapter:

"The surface of the earth changes. Some changes are due to slow processes such as erosion and weathering, and some changes are due to rapid processes such as landslides, volcanic eruptions, and earthquakes."
— **National Science Education Standards** (D3.A)

"Water's movements cause weathering and erosion, which change the land's surface features and create underground formations. Rainfall helps to shape the land and affects the types of living things found in a region. Water, ice, wind, living organisms, and gravity break rocks, soils, and sediments into smaller particles and move them around."
— **Next Generation Science Standards** (ESS2.A) (ESS2.C)

What You Learned

- Earth's surface is constantly changing.

- Some changes are very slow, like erosion or weathering.

- Some changes are very rapid, like landslides, volcanic eruptions, and earthquakes.

- Changes to Earth's surface may be harmful or helpful.

Weather & Seasons

Preview

Think about the weather in your area over the past year. Make a list of the different kinds of weather you've seen, especially weather extremes. Now look at your list. Most of the words and phrases you used were probably related in some way to measurable characteristics of precipitation, temperature, or wind speed and direction.

In this chapter, we'll not only explore how weather changes from day to day, but also why it changes from season to season. We'll also examine the role that precipitation, temperature, and wind play in the weather.

Essential Concepts

Weather is big part of our daily lives. No matter where you live on Earth, your local weather changes from day to day.* Some weather changes are almost too small to notice, but other weather changes are huge. For example, a cold snap on the Great Plains may drop temperatures more than fifty degrees in a few hours!

Weather also changes with the season. In temperate regions, the seasons are winter, spring, summer, and fall. These seasons are created by Earth's movement around the sun. Since the earth is tilted, the angle of sunlight hitting the earth changes over time. But how does sunlight angle affect the weather?

When sunlight is absorbed, heat is produced. Summer weather is warmer because sunlight hits the earth more directly. More

Yes, even in San Diego and Hawaii.

light is absorbed, producing more heat. But when sunlight hits the earth at an angle, it spreads out and less is absorbed. Winter weather is colder because sunlight hits the earth at more of an angle. Less light is absorbed, producing less heat.

Of course, during its twelve month journey around the sun, only one part of the earth tilts toward the sun at a time. That's why when it's summer in America, it's winter in Australia.

Since weather plays such an important role in our daily lives, we often talk about the weather. Weather words can be very specific. When someone uses a word like "blizzard" or "thunderstorm," you know just what kind of weather they mean.

Scientists describe weather by measurable characteristics like temperature, wind speed and direction, and precipitation. *Temperature* refers to a sense of hotness or coldness. For most of us, seventy degrees (fahrenheit) seems very comfortable. But temperatures over one hundred degrees feel much too hot, and temperatures below forty degrees feel much too cold.

Wind is how we commonly refer to air movement. We talk about how fast the wind is moving, or what direction it is coming from. In the winter, winds from the north may bring colder weather — but southerly winds might signal a warming trend.

Wind speed also helps us understand the weather. Predictions for a light breeze are very welcome on a hot, humid day. But high wind speeds can be a problem. Hurricanes and tornadoes contain high winds that can be very dangerous.

Precipitation refers to any form of water that falls to the earth's surface. Some examples include rain, snow, sleet, or hail. If snow is predicted, then you know to dress in warm clothing.* If rain is predicted, then you may want to carry an umbrella.

*and to break out the sleds and snow boards

Climate is a description of a region's typical weather conditions and the extent to which those conditions vary over years. The term can also be used to describe global weather conditions.

In recent years, one of the more hotly-debated political issues has been global climate change. Although a few scientists continue to claim global warming does not exist,* a study of 12,000 peer reviewed papers found almost ninety-eight percent of scientists not only endorse the view that climate change is occuring, but that human activity is one of the causes. More recently, the discussion appears to be moving from "does global warming exist" to "what should we do about it?"

Have Some Fun!

You'll need access to a detailed local weather source (newspaper, television, online etc.), and a way to keep accurate records (written or electronic). Record the date, time, temperature, barometric pressure, humidity, precipitation type, precipitation amount, wind direction, and wind speed at the same time each day. After recording daily readings for two weeks, review your data to see if you can spot patterns that might help you predict the weather. (Hint: check changes in barometric pressure.)

Have Some MORE Fun!

Bonus Activity 1:
Climate change is a serious issue. However, many people form their opinions based on talk show commentary rather than on factual data. NASA has provided a summary of major findings at: *http://climate.nasa.gov/evidence/*. After reading this information, review your opinion about climate change. (Don't let others do your thinking for you!)

*A few scientists still disagree about the negative health effects of smoking, too.

Bonus Activity 2:
Research variations in the climate for different parts of the world. Compare New Orleans, Louisiana with Fargo, North Dakota; Oslo, Norway with San Juan, Puerto Rico; Athens, Greece with Ottawa, Canada. How have people adapted to their specific climate? How might significant climate changes affect them?

National Standards

Here are the National Standards reflected in this chapter:

"Weather changes from day to day and over the seasons. Weather can be described by measurable quantities such as temperature, wind direction and speed, and precipitation. Seasons result from variations in the amount of the sun's energy hitting the surface, due to the tilt of the earth's rotation on its axis and the length of the day."
— **National Science Education Standards** (D3.B)

"Weather is the combination of sunlight, wind, snow or rain, and temperature in a particular region at a particular time. Scientists record patterns of weather across different times and areas so they can make predictions about what kind of weather might happen next. Climate describes a range of an area's typical weather conditions and the extent to which those conditions vary over years."
— **Next Generation Science Standards** (ESS2.D)

What You Learned

• The weather changes from day to day and over the seasons.

• Temperature, wind speed and direction, and precipitation help us describe the weather.

• Seasons are related to the earth's tilt and the length of the day.

• Climate change may significantly impact local weather.

Related
Science

"Anyone who has never made a mistake
has never tried anything new."

- Albert Einstein

Investigations

Preview

Scientific investigations always start with a question. Often the question is something about what, when, where, or how. Different questions require different kinds of investigations, and scientists are experts at matching investigations to questions.

Most of us are familiar with investigations that are based on experiments.* We'll explore that process in this chapter. But we'll also look at other types of scientific investigations that use different procedures.

Essential Concepts

As we said, a scientific investigation always starts with a question. For example, a scientist may want to know what a material is, or where it came from, or how it can be used.** Each of these questions requires a different kind of investigation that requires a different process.

Description is a basic form of scientific investigation. A scientist examines an object, an event, or an organism in great detail, then compares his/her findings with the findings of other scientists. Let's look at some examples:

Brian Mason, a New Zealand geochemist, was a pioneer in the study of meteorites and lunar rocks. He spent his life studying and describing these unique objects, and played a leading role in defining our understanding of the nature of the solar system.

*especially if the MythBusters shot a cannonball through your living room
**A lot of low-budget sci-fi movies are based on this theme.

Eddie Bernard, an American geophysicist, has focused much of his career on tsunami research. His detailed scientific descriptions of these dangerous waves and their causes has done much to influence public policy and save lives.

Jane Goodall, a Bristish anthropologist, is considered to be the world's foremost expert on chimpanzees. She spent forty-five years studying and describing the behavior of chimpanzees in Gombe Stream National Park in Tanzania.

Classification is another form of investigation. Classification involves placing an organism, an object, or an event into a specific scientific group.

In 2007, a small group of researchers discovered an ususual salamander in Georgia. After two years of careful study, biologists determined these salamanders were so distinct that they didn't fit any existing genus. They were classified as a new species, with the potential to change what scientists know about amphibians.

Hurricanes are classified by their wind strength. A "Category 5" hurricane has sustained winds of over 155 miles per hour! Since 2004, seven Atlantic storms have reached this strength, although most weakened before making landfall.

Occasionally a classification may change. In 2006, astronomers reclassifed Pluto from a planet to a dwarf planet.

Experiments are a well-known form of scientific investigation. Experiments allow scientists the opportunity to test their ideas to see if they are correct. Scientific fields like biology, chemistry, and physics rely on controlled experiments to constantly expand existing knowledge.

In the 1800s, a priest named Gregor Mendel studied plant characteristics by growing thousands of pea plants. Mendel's experiments discovered dominant and recessive traits, and became the foundation for today's science of genetics.

Also in the 1800s, scientist Louis Pasteur studied bacteria and molds, and conducted research on the process of fermentation. Pasteur's experiments helped prove germ theory, and led to the vaccines that protect millions of people and animals today.

In the late 1930s, a group of physicists at Columbia University conducted the first nuclear fission experiment in America. Members of this team went on to develop the first nuclear reactor, the foundation for today's nuclear power industry.

Whenever scientists conduct investigations, they must compare their answers to what other scientists know. Sharing data and methods helps verify that an investigation's conclusions are accurate. Scientific investigations are a vital part of learning about our world. Who knows what remarkable things are still waiting to be discovered?

Have Some Fun!

You'll need a small bowl, a paper plate, and a spoonful each of red beans, pinto beans, split peas, and lentils (dry). Place the materials in the bowl and mix thoroughly. Choose a specific characteristic (size, shape, color, etc.) and sort the material into piles accordingly. Record your results. Now repeat the process using a different characteristic. This activity models *classification*. Even though real scientific classification is much more complex and follows very precise rules, the process is similar.

Have Some MORE Fun!

Bonus Activity 1:
Place a clear glass half full of vinegar in a disposable cake pan. Set a spoonful of baking soda beside the pan. Ready? Now quickly dump the "white power" into the "clear liquid." There should be a sudden reaction between the two materials. This activity models using an *experiment* as a form of scientific investigation.

Bonus Activity 2:
Write a description of a dog you have known. Be as detailed as possible. Now write a description of a different dog. Compare the descriptions. Chances are that even though they're both "dogs" the descriptions are very different. This activity models using *description* as a form of scientific investigation.

National Standards

Here are the National Standards reflected in this chapter:

"Scientific investigations involve asking and answering a question and comparing the answer with what scientists already know about the world. Scientists use different kinds of investigations depending on the questions they are trying to answer."
— **National Science Education Standards** (A2.D) (A2.E)

"Asking questions, making observations, and gathering information are helpful in thinking about problems. Before beginning to design a solution, it is important to clearly understand the problem. Communicating with peers about proposed solutions is an important part of the design process, and shared ideas can lead to improved designs"
— **Next Generation Science Standards** (ETS1.A) (ETS1.B)

What You Learned

• A scientific investigation starts with asking a specific question.

• Different questions require different kinds of investigations.

• Types of investigations include describing objects, events, and organisms; classifying them; or conducting experiments.

• To verify accuracy, answers must be compared with what other scientists already know.

Preview

Think about something exciting you have seen. What did you do after you saw it? Who did you tell about it? What did they think about it? Sharing new information helps make things memorable and fun, and its one way that knowledge spreads.

Scientists use "scientific explanations" to share new information. By accurately documenting and sharing data and methods, a scientist allows his or her investigations to be repeated by other scientists.* This helps verify the findings, making certain that the conclusions are accurate. In this chapter, we'll take a closer look at how this works.

Essential Concepts

In the last chapter, you learned that scientists are constantly asking questions. They then attempt to answer these questions through scientific investigations.

But once an investigation is complete, a scientist needs to carefully explain what has been found. Scientific explanations are a way that scientists can describe the data collected and methods used, and compare their findings with existing knowledge.

For example, suppose you have three rocks — one is granite, one is sandstone, and one is pumice. Based on what you know about rocks, you might guess all of them will sink if you drop them in water. But good scientists test their theories. So you conduct an investigation by dropping each rock into an aquarium.**

*perhaps after hours on stormy nights, if your assistant's name is Igor
**much to the dismay of the angelfish!

117

The granite sinks. The limestone sinks. But the pumice floats! No matter how many times you try, it never sinks.

Based on your observations, you now can present evidence that pumice will not sink (at least not this particular piece of pumice). Then when you compare your findings to accepted theories, you discover that most pumice rocks float because they have air trapped inside.

A true scientific explanation always reflects this process in some fashion. It helps verify that the data is clear and can be repeated, and it also explains the relationship of the data to any accepted scientific theories.

Good scientific explanations are also extremely detailed. Scientists are careful to record anything that might vary. Let's look at our example again. We had three rocks, an aquarium, and some water. These were our primary variables.

But a thorough scientific explanation would describe each variable in detail. Details about the rocks would include things like shape, weight, and color. The explanation would also need to include the exact measurements of the aquarium, the depth and temperature of the water, and so on.

This careful attention to detail would allow other scientists to repeat the investigation exactly the way that you conducted it. By observing their results, these other scientists could then either support or counter your conclusions.

Carefully documenting your work, and sharing your data and methods is an imporant part of being a good scientist. It's also an excellent way to verify your specific conclusions are accurate.*

Here's another important benefit of scientific explanations: As scientists review the work of other scientists, they often find

and that you won't get "busted" on Mythbusters

new connections and ask new questions. This allows them to efficiently build on previous work, and move scientific knowledge forward more rapidly. Many of our greatest discoveries and inventions came about exactly because of this process.

In short, scientific explanations not only greatly expand our knowledge, but constantly lead to amazing new things!

Have Some Fun!

Write a scientific explanation for the *classification* investigation you conducted in the previous lesson (page 115). Describe what you observed, then document the data you collected and the methods you used. Compare the results of your first attempt to the results of your second attempt. If possible, have a friend review your findings.

Have Some MORE Fun!

Bonus Activity 1:
Write a scientific explanation for the *experiment* you conducted in the previous lesson (Bonus Activity 1, page 115). Describe what you observed, then document the data you collected and the methods you used. Compare the results to similar experiments you have seen. If possible, have a friend review your findings.

Bonus Activity 1:
Write a scientific explanation for the *description* investigation you conducted in the previous lesson (Bonus Activity 2, page 116). Describe what you observed, then document the data you collected and the methods you used. Compare the results to other references on dogs (books, Internet, etc.). If possible, have a friend review your findings.

National Standards

Here are the National Standards reflected in this chapter:

"Scientists develop explanations using observations (evidence) and what they already know about the world (scientific knowledge). Good explanations are based on evidence from investigations. Scientists make the results of their investigations public. They describe the investigations in ways that enable others to repeat the investigations."
— **National Science Education Standards** (A2.A) (A2.B)

"Science knowledge is based upon logical and conceptual connections between evidence and explanations. A scientific theory is a substantiated explanation of some aspect of the natural world, based on a body of facts that have been repeatedly confirmed through observation and experiment and the science community validates each theory before it is accepted. If new evidence is discovered that the theory does not accommodate, the theory is generally modified in light of this new evidence."
— **Next Generation Science Standards** (PS3.D) (PS4.A)

What You Learned

• Scientists develop explanations based on their investigations.

• Scientific explanations describe what has been observed.

• Scientific explanations also document the data collected and what methods were used.

• Scientific explanations should always include comparisons to existing knowledge.

• All scientific explanations must be reviewed by other scientists.

Instruments

Preview

Think about a time you were using a magnifying glass. What were you looking at? How did the magnifying glass help you? Now think about a time you used a thermometer or a ruler, and ask yourself the same questions.

Magnifiers, thermometers, and rulers are simple instruments that we use all the time. Scientists use special versions of these tools to greatly expand their ability to gain information. In this chapter, we'll take a closer look at scientific instruments.

Essential Concepts

Scientists are constantly investigating our world. What they see, hear, taste, touch, and smell tells them many things.* But if scientists were limited to using their five senses, most of our world would never be clearly understood or explained.

That's why scientists use various tools and instruments to help them gather more detailed and accurate information. Some of these instruments are very simple. Others are extremely complex. Different instruments are designed for different purposes.*

Simple scientific instruments include various kinds of magnifiers, thermometers, and rulers. Each of these tools helps extend our senses in some way.

A simple *magnifying glass* makes things look bigger so we can examine them more closely. A microscope magnifies objects

*like "don't touch that!"
**Check out the "rhinoscope" on page 123.

121

even more, helping us see things that are thousands of times smaller than a pinhead.

A telescope is another kind of magnifier, allowing us to observe objects throughout the solar system and beyond. Even reading glasses are a simple kind of magnifier, making print look larger so we can read more clearly.

Thermometers are another type of common instrument. Using a thermometer helps us accurately determine temperature. We often use thermometers to check the temperature outside, or to see if someone is running a fever.

But simple thermometers have a limited range, so scientists have created special thermometers for extreme temperatures. For example, a noise thermometer uses sound waves to measure extreme cold. Noise thermometers can measure temperatures far below zero.* A fiber optic thermometer uses light waves to measure extreme heat. Some fiber optic thermometers can measure temperatures as high as 4500 degrees!

Rulers are simple instruments, too. Rulers can be used to measure the length, width, or height of something. But like thermometers, simple rulers have a very limited range. So scientists have created special instruments that are designed to measure size extremes.

Lasers can be used to measure in "microns" — a very tiny unit of measurement. A human hair, for example, is about 60 microns wide. Radar signals use measurements based on the speed of light. They can be used to measure huge distances, like the space between planets.**

Even though some scientific instruments have complex names, you can often tell what they do by how the word ends. Words

Never lick a noise thermometer!
**although not the immeasurable distance between adolescence and adulthood*

that end in meter (like speedometer or barometer) are usually instruments that are designed to measure. Words that end in scope (like stereoscope or rhinoscope) are usually instruments that are used for detecting or viewing. And words that end in graph (like cardiograph or seismograph) are usually instruments for recording or displaying.

By extending the range of our senses, scientific instruments continue to lead to amazing new discoveries.

Have Some Fun!

You'll need a ruler, a 3-inch stick, a quarter, a book, a table, a shoe, and a way to keep records (written or electronic). Using the quarter, "measure" the book, the table, and the shoe. Record the results. (For example, the book might be "8 quarters" tall.) Now repeat using the stick as a measuring device. Again, record the results. Finally, use the ruler as a measuring device. You should end up with three standards (quarters, sticks, inches) for each item measured. The comparisons in this activity demonstrate the importance of measurement standards.

Have Some MORE Fun!

Bonus Activity 1:
Find a professional who works with microscopes. (Clinics and colleges are often good sources.) Ask him/her to demonstrate various types of microscopes. If possible, look at some slides. Discuss how microscopes are essential to his/her daily work.

Bonus Activity 2:
Have some fun dissecting scientific words. For instance, "rhinoscope" comes from the greek words for "nose" (rhino) and "to look at" (scope). Thus a rhinoscope is a device for looking up someone's nose! Research the origins of other complex scientific words, then share your findings with a friend.

National Standards

Here are the National Standards reflected in this chapter:

"Simple instruments, such as magnifiers, thermometers, and rulers provide more information than scientists can obtain using only their natural senses."
— **National Science Education Standards** (A2.C)

"Patterns in the natural world can be observed and measured in various ways. Scientists make observations from several sources and in several ways in order to construct an evidence-based account for natural phenomena."
— **Next Generation Science Standards** (ESS1.A) (ESS1.C)

What You Learned

• Scientific instruments help scientists gather more information.

• Scientific instruments range from very simple to very complex.

• Magnifiers make things easier for scientists to see.

• Thermometers help scientists determine accurate temperature.

• Rulers help scientists make more accurate measurements.

Index

Bill Who?

Bill Morelan has been a **Teacher of the Year** in two states, served as a consultant for several elementary curricula, was Publications Chair for the Arkansas Reading Association, and has been a popular speaker at educational conferences nationwide for over 20 years.

An experienced teacher, principal, and author, "Dr. Bill" has a passion for quality education ... a process he believes should not only be meaningful, but **FUN!**

In addition to his extensive experience in both public and private schools, Bill was a pioneer homeschooler — teaching his two daughters at home in the early 1980s. Both went on to achieve advanced degrees, and today one is a highly-respected elementary teacher, while the other is actively involved in the homeschool movement.

Bill teaches at the smallest high school in Arkansas (by choice). His "writer's den" is a restored 1958 Boles Aero travel trailer at Byrd's Adventure Center on the historic Mulberry River.

"I'm not crazy.
My mother had me tested."

– Dr. Sheldon Cooper

You have reached the end of the book.
I hope you enjoyed reading it as much as
I enjoyed writing it.

Now put it down and go outside!

Made in the USA
Middletown, DE
19 January 2024

48136575R00076